The Grenada Intervention

THE GRENADA INTERVENTION

Analysis and Documentation

William C. Gilmore

Facts on File Publications
New York, New York

Published by Facts on File, Inc.
460 Park Avenue South
New York, N.Y. 10016, U.S.A.

First published 1984 by Berlin Verlag
© William C. Gilmore 1984

Library of Congress Cataloging in Publication Data

Gilmore, William C.
  The Grenada Intervention
  Includes index
1. Intervention (International law).
2. Grenada – History – American invasion, 1983.
3. United States – Foreign relations – Grenada.
4. Grenada – Foreign relations – United States.
I. Title.
JX4481.G55   1984   341.5'8   84-9649

ISBN 0-87196-920-3

Typeset in West Germany
Printed and bound in Great Britain

CONTENT

ANALYSIS

PART I: THE GRENADA INTERVENTION: BACKGROUND
          AND ANATOMY

PART II: THE GRENADA INTERVENTION IN INTER-
          NATIONAL LAW

DOCUMENTATION

PREFACE

Throughout October and November 1983 I was based at the Cave Hill Campus of the University of the West Indies in Barbados. From this vantage point I followed, with a concern shared by all with whom I had contact, the developing political crisis in Grenada and the reactions to it in the eastern Caribbean and elsewhere. The present study is the consequence of those and subsequent observations.

The analysis of the international legal aspects of the armed intervention of October 1983 which follows is intended to be no more than introductory in nature and to draw only provisional conclusions. The necessarily incomplete nature of the factual information presently available to me dictates such an approach.

The documents which are reproduced within are, by way of contrast, intended to be of more lasting value. They are overwhelmingly West Indian in origin and it is hoped that the decision to make them available in this way will permit more comprehensive analysis of the legal and other issues involved to be undertaken by members of the scholarly community.

If this work, kindly and efficiently typed by Mrs. Eileen Wood, assists in provoking future debate and discussion of the complex legal issues surrounding this event then it will have served its modest purpose. I am pleased to acknowledge the kind financial assistance of the Carnegie Trust for the Universities of Scotland which made much of the relevant research possible.

Old College,
Edinburgh.
February, 1984.

William C. Gilmore
LL.B., LL.M., M.A.

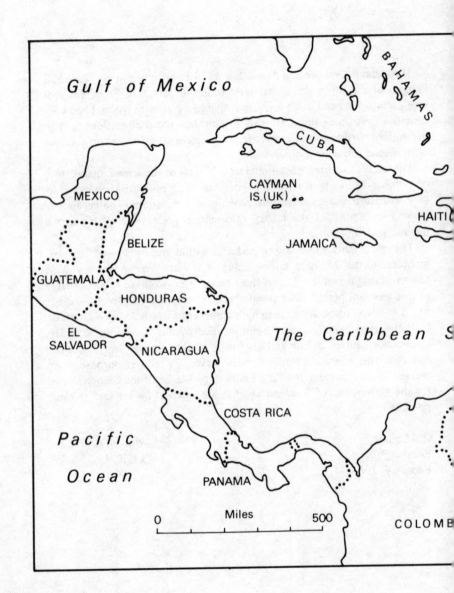

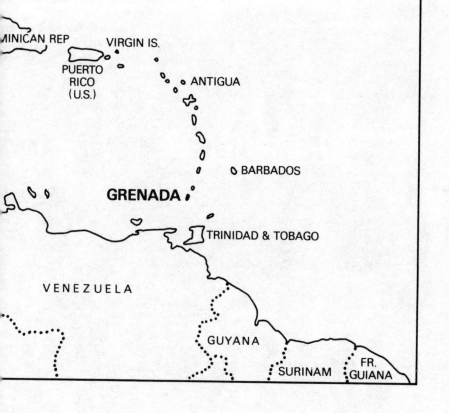

PART I
THE GRENADA INTERVENTION:
BACKGROUND AND ANATOMY

1. Introduction to a Micro-State

When, on the morning of 25 October 1983, elements of the United States' armed forces in conjunction with contingents from the security forces of a number of Caribbean nations[1] landed on the island of Grenada, one of the western hemispheres smallest and most obscure states became the temporary focus of world attention.[2]

The independent state of Grenada[3] is the final southern island in the volcanic inner arc of the Windward Islands, which, in turn, constitute part of the Lesser Antilles.[4] It is located some 144 km. north of Trinidad and some 106 km. south west of St. Vincent. In addition to the main island

---

1 Jamaica, Barbados, Antigua, Dominica, St. Lucia and St. Vincent. Forces from St. Christopher/Nevis were unable to participate immediately but subsequently became involved in the "peacekeeping" operation.

2 See, Part I (5) infra.

3 Grenada was discovered by Christopher Columbus in 1498 and was subsequently colonized by France. It became subject to British sovereignty, by cession, pursuant to the Treaty of Paris in 1763. Following further hostilities this status was confirmed by the Treaty of Versailles, 1783. See, K. Roberts-Wray, Commonwealth and Colonial Law (Stevens & Sons, London: 1966), at pp. 850—851. See also, Patchett, Reception of Law in the West Indies, (1972), Jamaica Law Journal, p. 17, at pp. 23—24. Grenada became an independent state on 7 Feb. 1974. See, Part I (2) infra.

4 See, H. Blume, The Caribbean Islands (Longman Group Ltd., London: 1974), at pp. 350—353.

11

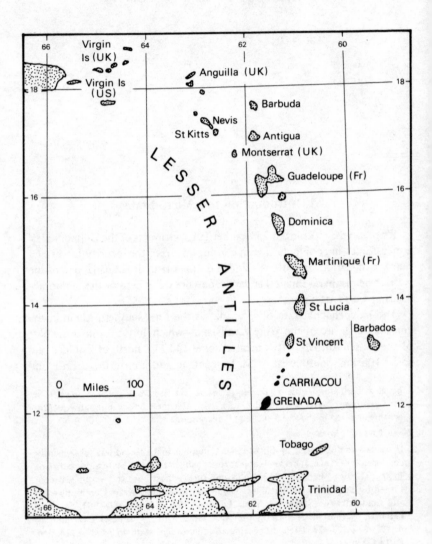

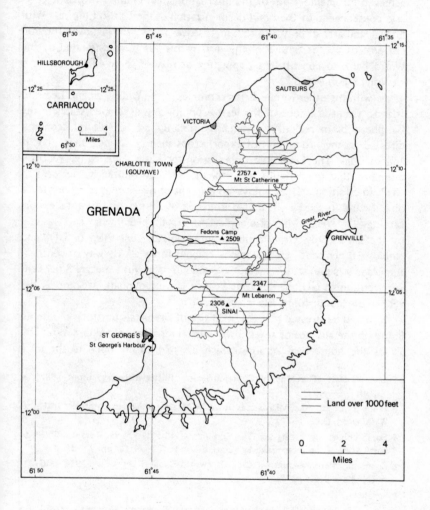

61°30' · HILLSBOROUGH · 12°25' · 12°25' · CARRIACOU · 0 Miles 4 · 61°30'

61°45' · 61°40' · 61°35' · 12°15'

SAUTEURS

VICTORIA

CHARLOTTE TOWN (GOUYAVE) · 12°10' · 12°10'

2757 ▲ Mt St Catherine

GRENADA

Great River

Fedons Camp ▲ 2509 · GRENVILLE

2347 · Mt Lebanon · 12°05' · 12°05'

2306 ▲ SINAI

ST GEORGE'S · St George's Harbour

Land over 1000 feet

0 · 2 · 4 · Miles

12°00'

61°50' · 61°45' · 61°40'

the land territory of the state includes a number of islets of which the largest is Carriacou.[5]

Grenada is one of a relatively large number of micro-states[6] which have achieved full membership of the international community in recent years as a consequence of the rapid decolonization of the British Empire.[7] With a total land area of only 344 sq. km. it strives to support just over 100,000 citizens. Given the nature of the terrain this has been estimated by the World Bank to constitute a population density of some 448 persons per sq. km. of arable land.[8]

As with the other former British colonies in the Windward and Leeward Islands, Grenada is one of the least economically developed states in the Caribbean basin region.[9] It remains primarily an agricultural economy directed to the production of export crops such as nutmeg, mace, cocoa and bananas. The Economic Commission for Latin America has recently estimated that the agricultural sector in 1981 contributed 32 per cent to GDP. In addition, "[i]t employs 28 per cent of the employed labour force directly and in 1981 contributed in excess of 28 per cent of total export earnings".[10] Tourism has also achieved a certain prominence and was said by the same study "to contribute approximately one-third of GDP and employ 10 per cent of the employed labour force".[11] By way of contrast, the island's manufacturing sector was able to offer but a meagre 3 per cent contribution to GDP in the same year.[12] Unemployment, at some 27 per cent of the labour force, is a major problem.[13]

It should be stressed that the small size of Grenada's territory and population, in the absence of any known mineral resources of value, severely restricts the number of options which are realistically open to the local

5 See, W. Dale, The Modern Commonwealth (Butterworths, London: 1983), at p. 230.

6 See, e.g., E. Plischke, Microstates in World Affairs (American Enterprise Institute, Washington, D.C.: 1977).

7 For a convenient listing see, The Commonwealth: Its Special Responsibilities to Small States (Commonwealth Secretariat, London: 1979), at pp. 29–30.

8 Economic Memorandum on Grenada (World Bank (Report No. 1994 – GRD) Washington, D.C.: 1978).

9 See, id.

10 Economic Activity 1981 in Caribbean Countries (Economic Commission for Latin America (CEPAL/CARIB 82/10), Port-of-Spain: 1982), Pt. VII, p. 2.

11 Id. p. 9.

12 See, id., at p. 5.

13 See, id., at p. 7.

government. For the same reason Grenada shares a number of economic characteristics with her small island state neighbours. For instance, industrialization is impeded by small market size and insufficient numbers of skilled and high-level manpower. Furthermore, "[d]iseconomies of small size result in disproportionately high per capita cost infrastructure and administrative and social services".[14] The need to maintain highly open economies leaves these states particularly sensitive to fluctuations in international prices and demand. In 1982 a United Kingdom House of Commons Select Committee summarized the economic circumstances of Grenada and the other smaller eastern Caribbean islands in these words:

"All these territories have a narrow economic base, often relying on one crop, such as bananas; are heavily dependent on agricultural exports for their foreign exchange earnings and therefore are hard hit by the world recession; have high unemployment and poor levels of infrastructural development; lack local capital for investment and depend on external finance for a large proportion of their public investment. Moreover, they have to pay high prices for their energy imports, which are not matched by the returns on their exports, and so run into worsening balance of payments problems. Finally, they have increasing difficulties in meeting the cost of their relatively well-developed educational and health services."[15]

2. The Decolonization of Grenada

Throughout the 1940s and 1950s, the related themes of size and viability of colonial possessions dominated the thinking of both British authorities and West Indian political leaders[16], with federation of the islands viewed as a logical precondition for the attainment of independence.[17] A plan for a Federation of the West Indies, including Grenada,

14 S. Lestrade, CARICOM's Less Developed Countries (Institute of Social and Economic Research, University of the West Indies, Barbados: 1981), at. p. 8.

15 Foreign Affairs Committee, Caribbean and Central America (House of Commons Paper 47, 1981–82), at para. 142.

16 See, Lewis, The Commonwealth Caribbean and Self-Determination in the International System, in: V.A. Lewis (ed.), Size, Self-Determination and International Relations: The Caribbean (Institute of Social and Economic Research, University of the West Indies, Jamaica: 1976), p. 227, at p. 229.

17 See, Coard, The Meaning of Political Independence in the Commonwealth Caribbean, in: Independence for Grenada: Myth or Reality? (Institute of International Relations, University of the West Indies, Trinidad), at pp. 69–70. See also, R. Preis-

was finally implemented in 1958, but failed for a variety of reasons and was dissolved in 1962.[18]

By 1962, however, perspectives on the independence issue had undergone major transformations both in London and within the region. Jamaica became a full member of the international community in 1962, and was followed later in the same year by Trinidad and Tobago. Consequently, the political future of the various territories was no longer seen as being necessarily tied to a federated structure.[19]

Representatives of the governments of eight Caribbean territories, of which Grenada was one, met in Barbados in March of 1962 to discuss the future status of the islands and opted for the creation of a "truncated" federation in the eastern Caribbean.[20] Detailed proposals were then submitted to London. In April of 1962, the Secretary of State informed the British House of Commons that Her Majesty's Government viewed the proposal for a new federation as the best constitutional solution for the problems of the area. This announcement was followed by another constitutional conference in London, where the proposals were discussed in detail and finally agreed upon in May of 1962. The constitutional arrangements formulated at that time have proven to be, in one observer's words, "the high water mark of the federal scheme".[21]

Several factors were responsible for the declining fortunes of a federal solution for the islands. First, the Treasury in London was slow to respond to requests for financial assistance. Second, the consensus among the territories as to their future began to deteriorate. Grenada opted out of the federal scheme and made an unsuccessful attempt to unite politically with Trinidad. Subsequently, Antigua decided to leave the arrangement as a result of a disagreement with Britain over the question of common services and the fate of the island's Post Office. Montserrat also abandoned the plan. The last nail in the federation's coffin came in August of 1965 when

werk (ed.), Documents on International Relations in the Caribbean (Institute of Caribbean Studies, Universidad de Puerto Rico, Puerto Rico: 1970), at pp. 260—285.

18 For a detailed analysis of the federal experiment see, J. Mordecai, The West Indies: Federal Negotiations (1968). See also, Springer, Federation in the Caribbean: An Attempt that Failed, in: D. Lowenthal and L. Comitas (eds.), The Aftermath of Sovereignty (Anchor Press/ Doubleday, New York: 1973), pp. 189—213.

19 See, Coard, supra., note 17, at p. 70.

20 See, Lewis, The Agony of the Eight, in: D. Lowenthal and L. Comitas, op. cit., p. 215, at p. 223.

21 Id., at p. 225.

Barbados announced that it intended to seek independence because the opportunity to achieve early independence through the federation appeared slight.[22]

With the demise of the federation, the British authorities found themselves confronted by a problem to which neither independence nor traditional formulae of colonial government seemed an appropriate response. Whitehall felt the necessity of devising a new set of constitutional status proposals which would placate the "Committee of Twenty-Four" at the United Nations as well as meet the demands from local leaders for greater political control and authority. Consequently, the Secretary of State convened a conference at Oxford in the summer of 1965.[23] In contrast to normal constitutional conference procedure, no elected representatives from the Caribbean territories were invited to attend. From this meeting the basic outlines of a new constitutional experiment, to be tested in the decolonization "laboratory" of the Caribbean, evolved: statehood in association with the mother country.

The Oxford outline was subject to further internal discussion and refinement in London in the months that followed. In November of 1965, the Colonial Office sent representatives to Antigua, Dominica, Grenada, St. Kitts/Nevis/Anguilla, St. Lucia, and St. Vincent to present the new plan. In light of these discussions, a memorandum outlining the constitutional scheme was prepared.[24]

The core of the new formula consisted of three proposals. First, the island territories would be given virtually complete autonomy in their internal affairs based on a Westminster-type constitutional model which could be amended locally. Second, the individual territories would be given the power to terminate the status of association unilaterally and move on to full sovereign statehood should they so desire. Third, the United Kingdom would remain responsible for the exercise of power and authority in the spheres of citizenship, external affairs and defence, retaining the necessary executive and legislative power to carry out these tasks fully.

After months of diplomatic reflection and public debate, three constitutional conferences were called to discuss the proposals in detail: one for Antigua, one for delegations from the Windward Islands, including Grenada[25], and one for St. Kitts/Nevis/Anguilla. Local political leaders partici-

22 Report of the Barbados Constitutional Conference, Cmnd. 3058 (1966), at p. 3.

23 See, 740 Parl. Deb., H.C. (5th ser.) 337 (1967).

24 See generally, Constitutional Proposals for Antigua, St. Kitts/Nevis/Anguilla, Dominica, St. Lucia, St. Vincent, Grenada. Cmnd. 2865 (1965).

25 The Grenada delegation which attended this Conference was headed by Chief

pated fully (including opposition members from the legislatures) with each Chief Minister playing a crucial role. An examination of the conference reports reveals that in the discussions which ensued the British authorities still had to press for acceptance of their proposals. This is most clearly reflected in the Windward Islands report where the Secretary of State was asked to consider the alternative of granting full internal self-government along the lines of a more traditional colonial formula.[26]

Ultimately, the Oxford scheme was accepted by Grenada and the other islands as the best plan that could be obtained under the circumstances, and arrangements were made to bring it into effect in early 1967. Given the novel nature of the proposed measure, it was deemed necessary to obtain statutory authorisation from Parliament and the West Indies Act of 1967 was enacted for this purpose.[27]

Based to a considerable extent on the relationship existing in the south west Pacific between New Zealand and the Cook Islands[28], the initial British hope was that the status of associated statehood[29] would take on a quality of permanence. For a variety of reasons, extensively treated elsewhere[30], it was not long before local political leaders began to reassess the option of moving on to full independence. Following the Grenada general election of 1972, at which the subject of independence was a major issue, the government of the Premier, Mr. (now Sir) Eric Gairy, pressed the United Kingdom to terminate their remaining responsibilities for the governance of the territory. In May of 1973 a constitutional conference was convened

Minister Blaize. Mr. Gairy, who opposed many aspects of the new arrangements, attended as Leader of the Opposition. See generally, Cmnd. 3021 (1966).

26 See, id., at pp. 6—7.

27 1967, c.4 (U.K.).

28 See, e.g., A. Leibowitz, Colonial Emancipation in the Pacific and the Caribbean (Praeger, New York: 1976), at pp. 132—146.

29 See, Broderick, Associated Statehood — A New Form of Decolonisation, (1968) 17: International and Comparative Law Quarterly, pp. 368—403; Forbes, The West Indies Associated States: Some Aspects of the Constitutional Arrangements, (1970) 19: Social and Economic Studies, pp. 57—88; and, Gilmore, The Associated States of the Commonwealth Caribbean: The Constitutions and the Individual, (1979) 11: Lawyer of the Americas, pp. 1—41. See also, J. Crawford, The Creation of States in International Law (Clarendon Press, Oxford: 1979), pp. 370—377.

30 For the views of the author see, Gilmore, Legal Perspectives on Associated Statehood in the Eastern Caribbean, (1979) 19: Virginia Journal of International Law, pp. 489—555, and Gilmore, Requiem for Associated Statehood? (1982) 8: Review of International Studies, pp. 9—25.

in London to discuss the question[31] and, in spite of growing social unrest and opposition from other political groupings within the island[32], this request was granted. On 7 February 1974 Grenada became an independent state whithin the Commonwealth.[33] Given that internal autonomy had been granted in 1967, few major constitutional changes were considered to be necessary[34] and the formal aspect of the transition found expression primarily in the acquisition of full responsibility for external affairs, defence and citizenship matters.

3. Post-Independence Developments

Independence for Grenada was not an occasion for rejoicing as political unrest and civil disturbances continued. Writing only a few weeks before the event Ryan was to remark that:

"Threats to life and limb, looting and destruction of property in the capital city, seem to have become commonplace. The only other 'Caribbean' state which has had to endure a comparable measure of open political conflict involving violence on the eve of independence was Guyana."[35]

Some measure of internal stability was subsequently imposed by the increasingly repressive, though pro-western, government of Prime Minister Gairy. It is widely acknowledged that the activities of his government left much to be desired.[36] As a recent report of the British House of Commons Select Committee on Foreign Affairs was to state, "it is generally agreed that it was corrupt, repressive and sustained only by rigged elections, and that it grossly mismanaged the economy".[37] Gairy himself was an eccentric figure who, in the recent words of the United States Information Agency, "combined flamboyant populism and strong-arm tactics with interest in unidentified flying objects and unconventional religion".[38]

31 See, The Grenada Constitutional Conference 1973, Cmnd. 5379 (1973).

32 See, e.g., Smith, A Summary of Some Important Political Events in Grenada from 1951 to March 13, 1979, (1979) 5: Bulletin of Eastern Caribbean Affairs, No. 1, p. 11, at pp. 15—16.

33 See, supra., note 5, at p. 231.

34 For the independence constitution see, S.I. 1973, No. 2155, (U.K.).

35 See, Independence for Grenada: Myth or Reality?, supra., note 17, at p. 1.

36 See, e.g., Grenada: The Peaceful Revolution (EPICA, Washington, D.C.: 1982), at pp. 42—50.

37 Supra., note 15, at para. 113.

38 Grenada: Background and Facts (United States Information Agency, Washington,

Given the above it was not entirely surprising when on 13 March, 1979 the Grenada regime became the first Commonwealth Caribbean government to be overthrown by force of arms. Among the leaders of this near bloodless coup were Mr. Maurice Bishop, then leader of the Opposition in Parliament and a leading personality in the New Jewel Movement[39], and Mr. Hudson Austin who commanded the small military force (People's Revolutionary Army) which quickly obtained the surrender of units loyal to the Gairy administration.[40]

This grouping moved swiftly to suspend the existing independence constitution[41] and to declare the establishment of a People's Revolutionary Government (PRG)[42] in which was vested "all executive and legislative power".[43] Somewhat unusually for a revolutionary government, the decision was also taken that Grenada would retain the status of a monarchy within the Commonwealth and that the position of Governor-General would be retained. Thus, on 25 March 1979 People's Law (the given designation for enactments of the new regime) number 3 was promulgated. It reads in full thus:

"The Head of State shall remain Her Majesty the Queen and her representative in this country shall continue to be the Governor-General who shall perform such functions as the People's Revolutionary Government may from time to time advise."

The PRG also acted expeditiously, as Burgess has noted, to establish "a substantial measure of control over the judiciary".[44] In this context

D.C.: 1983), at p. 3. For an account of Gairy's rise to power see, A. Singham, The Hero and the Crowd in a Colonial Polity (Yale University Press, New Haven: 1968).

39 A 1973 merger between the Jewel Movement (Joint Endeavour for Welfare, Education and Liberation) and MAP (Master Assembly for the People).

40 See, H.A.F., Grenada: The Sovereignty of a People, (1979): West Indian Law Journal, p. 3, at p. 3.

41 It was proclaimed that: "The Constitution of Grenada is hereby and has been suspended as of 12.01 a.m. on March 13th, 1979. All acts and/or deeds by or under the authority of the People's Revolutionary Government (PRG) are hereby deemed and declared to have been legally done and shall not be called into question in any Court of Law or otherwise." Grenada People's Law, No. 1 (1979).

42 See, the text of the Declaration of the Grenada Revolution at Appendix No. 1.

43 Grenada People's Law, No. 2 (1979). As Alexis has noted: "In no form of government in any Commonwealth Caribbean country other than Grenada does the same body of persons wield all executive as well as all legislative power." F. Alexis, Changing Caribbean Constitutions (Antilles Publications, Bridgetown, Barbados: 1983), p. 109.

44 Burgess, Law and the "Revolution": A Review of Post-Revolution Laws in Grenada, (1981) 7: Bulletin of Eastern Caribbean Affairs, No. 1, p. 20, at. p. 21.

Grenada withdrew from the existing sub-regional Supreme Court[45], which it shared with a number of other Commonwealth Caribbean territories, abolished appeals to the Privy Council[46] and established a Supreme Court of Grenada. This consists of a High Court and Court of Appeal[47] the membership of which can be effectively controlled by government.[48]

Neighbouring Commonwealth Caribbean governments were concerned by the course of events in Grenada and particularly by the manner in which power had been assumed.[49] Following a meeting of the independent Commonwealth Caribbean states in Barbados on 14 March 1979 a communiqué was issued. It reads in part:

"Ministers noted that these recent events had led to an overthrow of the Government of Grenada and that this was contrary to the traditional method of changing governments in the region. Ministers affirmed that the affairs of Grenada are for the people of that territory to decide and that accordingly there should be not outside interference. They, however, felt that the wider interests and unity of the area and of Grenada in particular require a return to constitutionality as soon as possible."[50]

Although this unease was compounded, for the more conservative governments, by the socialist orientation of the PRG, formal recognition followed speedily. Thus, "[o]n March 20 the governments of Barbados, Guyana and Jamaica declared their recognition of the new Government of Grenada".[51] The question of recognition did not arise either for Trinidad, which adheres to the Estrada doctrine, or for the United Kingdom, which took the view that the retention of the Governor-General in post rendered such action unnecessary. The above Commonwealth Caribbean initiative was swiftly imitated by, among others, the United States, Canada and Cuba.[52]

45 See, Grenada People's Law No. 4 (1979). Formerly known as the West Indies Associated States Supreme Court, this institution survives under the name of the Eastern Caribbean Supreme Court. See, The St. Lucia Constitution Order 1978, S.I. 1978, No. 1901 (U.K.), Sched. 2, s. 8. For the background see, Gilmore, supra., note 29, at pp. 15—16.

46 See, Grenada People's Law No. 84 (1979). For the background to the original retention of the Privy Council see, e.g., Gilmore, id., at pp. 17—19.

47 See, Grenada People's Law No. 4 (1979).

48 See, Grenada People's Law No. 14 (1979). See also, supra., note 44, at p. 21.

49 See, Gonsalves, The Importance of the Grenada Revolution to the Eastern Caribbean, (1979) 5: Bulletin of Eastern Caribbean Affairs, No. 1., p. 1, at p. 7. See also, supra., note 36, at pp. 56—58.

50 Text reproduced in supra., note 15, at p. 287.

51 Supra., note 40, p. 3.

52 See, id.

Local concern over the situation in Grenada did not, however, diminish significantly with the passage of time. In Barbados[53] and in other neighbouring Commonwealth states anxiety and frustration continued to be expressed concerning such issues as the failure of the PRG to hold elections, its disinclination to bring political detainees to trial, and its reluctance to permit any true expression of the doctrine of freedom of the press and other media.[54]

Serious disquiet was also aroused by the nature of the foreign policy formulated and pursued by the government of Prime Minister Bishop. Here the socialist direction of that government found its most concrete expression. As Gill was to comment in 1981:

"The People's Revolutionary Government (PRG) stresses its anti-imperialist position and identification with socialist goals, a commitment to internationalism and the need to buttress revolutionary solidarity, particularly with Cuba and Nicaragua, the former being Grenada's closest friend and ally."[55]

In pursuance of this policy Grenada rapidly expanded its diplomatic network beyond the leftist states of the region to include the Soviet Union, many of the countries of eastern Europe and third world states of a socialist orientation.[56] Sources of bilateral assistance were similarly diversified and came to embrace such non-traditional donors as Iraq, Algeria, the Soviet Union and East Germany. The aid relationship with Cuba developed swiftly, eventually "covering arms supplies . . ., health, fisheries, airport construction, education and cultural exchange".[57]

This radical change of emphasis found expression in international fora such as the United Nations. For example, "in January 1980 Grenada was the only state in the Commonwealth Caribbean to join with Cuba in voting against the United Nations resolution condemning the Soviet invasion of Afghanistan".[58] It became increasingly difficult, as Thorndike has noted,

---

53 See, e.g., Barriteau, Regional Comments: Barbados — Grenada Relations, (1980) 6: Bulletin of Eastern Caribbean Affairs, No. 5, at pp. 22–30.

54 See, e.g., A. Payne, Change in the Commonwealth Caribbean (Royal Institute of International Affairs, London: 1981), at p. 17.

55 Gill, The Foreign Policy of the Grenada Revolution, (1981) 7: Bulletin of Eastern Caribbean Affairs, No. 1., p. 1., at p. 1.

56 See, id.

57 See, Thorndike, The Grenada Revolution, its Effects and British Policy, in: supra., note 15, p. 164, at p. 167.

58 Supra., note 54, at p. 17.

to identify any issue "on which the PRG's position is at variance with that of Cuba or, for that matter, the Soviet Union".[59]

This seemingly radical shift in foreign policy, however, did not prevent Grenada from continuing to play a full part in the Commonwealth Caribbean's economic and political integration movement.[60] Thus, the PRG, following assurances given only two days after coming to power, remained as an active participant in the Caribbean Community and Common Market (CARICOM).[61] In addition to the Common Market, which contains a special regime for the so-called Less Developed Countries (LDC's) including Grenada[62], CARICOM's activities include functional or non-economic co-operation and the co-ordination of the foreign policies of the independent member states.[63]

Similarly, at the sub-regional level Grenada retained its existing institutional ties with the other LDC's of the eastern Commonwealth Caribbean (St. Christopher/Nevis, Antigua, Montserrat, Dominica, St. Lucia and St. Vincent). It thus remained within economic and financial institutions, such as the East Caribbean Common Market (ECCM)[64] and East Caribbean

59 Supra., note 57, at p. 167.

60 See generally, Carnegie, Commonwealth Caribbean Regionalism, (1979): Year Book of World Affairs, pp. 180—200.

61 Members include Belize, Jamaica, St. Christopher/Nevis, Antigua, Barbados, Montserrat, Dominica, St. Lucia, St. Vincent, Grenada, Trinidad and Tobago, and Guyana. The Bahamas was admitted as a member of the Community but not of the Common Market in July 1983. See, Communiqué: Fourth Meeting of the Conference of Heads of Government of the Caribbean Community, (1983) 9: Bulletin of Eastern Caribbean Affairs, No. 3, p. 27, at pp. 27—28. For a legal analysis of CARICOM see generally, H. Geiser, P. Alleyne and C. Gajraj, Legal Problems of Caribbean Integration (Sijthoff, Leyden: 1976). See also, Geiser, Regional Integration in the Commonwealth Caribbean, (1976) 10: Journal of World Trade Law, pp. 546—565; O'Connell, The Caribbean Community: Economic Integration in the Commonwealth Caribbean, (1976) 11: Journal of International Law and Economics, pp. 35—66; and, Dundas, The Law of the Caribbean Community, (1980): West Indian Law Journal, pp. 13—30.

62 See, e.g., Pollard, Institutional and Legal Aspects of the Caribbean Community, Vol. 14: Caribbean Studies, at. pp. 69—72. For a recent evaluation of this regime see, Goodwin and Lake, The LDC's in Integration Schemes: The CARICOM Experience, in: B. Ince, A. Bryan, H. Addo and R. Ramsaran (eds.), Issues in Caribbean International Relations (Institute of International Relations, University of the West Indies, Trinidad: 1983), at pp. 129—157.

63 See, W.G. Demas, West Indian Nationhood and Caribbean Integration (CCC Publishing House, Bridgetown, Barbados: 1974), at pp. 33—34.

64 See, e.g., A.J. Payne, The Politics of the Caribbean Community 1961—1979

Currency Authority (ECCA)[65], and did not withdraw from the more political consultative mechanism provided in the form of the West Indies (Associated States) Council of Ministers (WISA).[66]

Far from questioning its commitment to the integration movement the PRG actively participated in deepening the process. For example, on 18 June 1981 Prime Minister Bishop signed the Treaty Establishing the Organisation of Eastern Caribbean States (OECS).[67] This provided for greater co-operation in the sphere of foreign policy and co-ordination of collective defence and security arrangements, as well as promoting deeper economic integration.[68] Under this treaty the ECCM Secretariat, sited in Antigua, became the Economic Affairs Division of OECS.[69] In July of 1983 Grenada joined with its LDC neighbours in establishing the Eastern Caribbean Central Bank (ECCB).[70] This was effectively an upgrading of the existing, and often criticised, ECCA arrangements. It was designed, among other things, to entrust the institution with new functions and to equip it with monetary instruments to regulate the availability of money and credit in a manner consistent with the balanced growth and development of the economies of the participating territories.[71]

Grenada did not, however, become a party to the 29 October 1982 Memorandum of Understanding Relating to Security and Military Co-operation concluded between Antigua, Barbados, Dominica, St. Lucia and St. Vincent.[72] This brought into effect what has become known as the Re-

(Manchester University Press, Manchester: 1980), at p. 106. For the relationship between ECCM and CARICOM see, H. Geiser et al, supra., note 61, at pp. 55–56.

65 For an evaluation of this grouping see, A. McClean, Money and Banking in the East Caribbean Currency Area (Institute of Social and Economic Research, University of the West Indies, Jamaica: 1975). See also, "Some Aspects of Central Banking" (unpublished study dated 10 Nov. 1977 by ECCA, Basseterre, St. Kitts).

66 See, W. Axline, Caribbean Integration: The Politics of Regionalism (Frances Pinter Ltd., London: 1979), at p. 100.

67 Substantial sections of the treaty text are reproduced at Appendix No. 2. See also, Organisation of Eastern Caribbean States Law 1981, Grenada People's Law No. 41 (1981).

68 The author is in the course of preparing an analysis of the OECS treaty for publication in 1985.

69 (1981) 15: Caribbean Monthly Bulletin, No. 7, at p. 42.

70 For the text see, Eastern Caribbean Central Bank Agreement Act 1983, St. Lucia, Act No. 23 (1983).

71 See, East Caribbean Currency Authority: Annual Report and Statement of Accounts for the Year Ended 31st March 1982, at p. 20.

72 Substantial extracts from the text are reproduced at Appendix No. 4.

24

gional Security System.[73] Paragraph 2 of the agreement reflects the broad area in which co-operation was envisaged. It is worded as follows:

"The parties hereto agree to prepare contingency plans and assist one another on request in national emergencies, prevention of smuggling, search and rescue, immigration control, fishery protection, customs and excise control, maritime policing duties, protection of off-shore installations, pollution control, natural and other disasters and threats to national security."

The conclusion of this arrangement must be viewed as underlining the security worries of the participating eastern Caribbean states stemming, in part at least, from the nature of the change in government in Grenada in 1979 and the growing warmth of its relationship with countries within the Soviet sphere of influence.[74]

4. The United States and the Grenada Revolution

The United States has a lengthy history of interest in the Caribbean. The region, often thought of as America's "back yard", has for long been regarded by it as of vital importance. Successive U.S. governments have, in effect, seen the Caribbean sea as an American lake and acted accordingly.[75] As Martin has recently noted, "our reputation for imperialism, until Vietnam, rested largely on our military interventions in the Caribbean".[76]

The strength of this traditional American concern with the region can be regarded as a reflection of a number of interrelated factors. First, the Caribbean has since independence been considered as vital to U.S. national security. This view was, in turn, reinforced first by the project and later by the reality of the Panama Canal. Second, it has not insignificant economic interests in the region both in terms of direct investment and trade. As to the latter, "nearly one-half of United States trade and two-thirds of its oil imports pass through the Gulf of Mexico or the Panama Canal".[77] Third,

---

73 See, (1982) 10: Caribbean Monthly Bulletin, No. 10, p. 12, and No. 11, p. 29. For extracts from the text see, Appendix No. 4.

74 Certain post-independence developments in Dominica and St. Lucia had also contributed to an increased security consciousness within the sub-region.

75 See, Gordon, The United States and the Caribbean, in: E. de Kadt (ed.), Patterns of Foreign Influence in the Caribbean (Oxford University Press, London: 1972), p. 170, at pp. 171–172.

76 J. Martin, U.S. Policy in the Caribbean (Westview Press, Boulder: 1978), at p. 5.

77 Supra., note 15, at para. 189.

the United States is itself very much a Caribbean nation. In addition to the dependencies of Puerto Rico and the Virgin Islands, the States of Florida, Alabama, Mississippi, Louisiana and Texas all border on the Caribbean sea: "a great arc sweeping from Brownsville to Miami that is approximately equal to our Atlantic or our Pacific coastline".[78]

Historically, however, this American interest in the island states of the Caribbean has tended to focus on Cuba, the Dominican Republic and Haiti.[79] By way of contrast, "concern for the Commonwealth Caribbean has not generally been a high priority for the Americans, who continued to regard these states as a British preserve even during the 1960s and early 1970s, when it was apparent that Britain's interest in the Caribbean was waning fast. Certainly, little attention was paid to the problems of this part of the region by the Nixon and Ford administrations".[80] Indeed, given the lessening of tensions then evident between east and west, with a consequent diminution in the perceived nature of the Cuban threat, the Caribbean became for a time a subject of U.S. governmental neglect. As a senior State Department spokeswoman was to admit in 1978, "in the early seventies, in the absence of fears, we seldom focused our eyes on the Caribbean to any meaningful degree".[81]

This stance was quickly altered with the assumption of power by President Carter. Under his leadership the focus on Caribbean affairs was sharpened and the traditional reach of policy and interest extended to include the recently independent Commonwealth Caribbean states. A number of factors can be seen to have contributed to this shift. First, there was a growing awareness in Washington that the relative political tranquility of the region was likely to come under increasing strain. The pace of decolonization in the area, illustrated by the creation of a relatively large number of micro-states, and the consequent British political withdrawal from the area, was viewed as a potential threat to regional stability.[82] Furthermore,

78 Supra., note 76, at p. 8.

79 See, e.g., W. Perkins, Constraint of Empire: The United States and Caribbean Interventions (Clio Press, Oxford: 1981).

80 Supra., note 54, at p. 31. Much the same can be said of the U.S. attitude to the Caribbean possessions of France and the Netherlands. See, e.g., Gastman, Continental Europe and the Caribbean: The French and Dutch Experience, in: R. Millett and W. Will (eds.), The Restless Caribbean: Changing Patterns of International Relations (Praeger Publishers, London: 1979), at pp. 219—233.

81 Shelton, United States Policy Towards the Caribbean: A View from Washington, (1978) 4: International Trade Law Journal, p. 173, at p. 174.

82 See, e.g., Laing, Independence and Islands: The Decolonization of the British Caribbean, (1979) 12: International Law and Politics, at pp. 281—312.

it was widely felt in the new administration that the serious economic difficulties faced by Caribbean states were being compounded by the severe impact of rising oil prices and inflation. These pressures were seen to threaten the Caribbean's democratic institutions and to provide possible avenues for the expansion of communist influence.[83] Under Carter, therefore, American development assistance to the region was substantially increased and his administration played a significant role in the creation of the Caribbean Group for Co-operation in Economic Development. This grouping brought together, under the World Bank, representatives from international institutions and over thirty countries to promote regional economic development.[84]

At a more politically controversial level, the United States concluded two new treaties relating to the status and security of the Panama Canal.[85] Carter also initiated a number of modest moves, including the establishment of diplomatic "interest sections", designed to lessen tension and increase dialogue with Cuba.[86]

In spite of the latter, the Carter administration shared with its predecessors a constant concern over any increase of Cuban (and hence Soviet) influence within the Caribbean.[87] Indeed, it is this traditional fear of communist expansion in its "back yard" which, in large measure, accounts for the extremely cool American response to the socialist Grenada revolution of March, 1979. By way of illustration, it has been reported that on 9 April of that year the U.S. Ambassador, based in Barbados, informed the new leader of Grenada that:

"Although my government recognizes your concerns over allegations of a possible counter-coup, it also believes that it would not be in Grenada's

83 See, e.g., text of remarks made by President Carter on 9 April 1980. Reproduced in: Current Policy, No. 174 (U.S. Dept. of State).

84 See, e.g., text of address by Ambassador Habib to the Miami Conference on the Caribbean, 28 Nov., 1979 (typed text provided by U.S. Dept. of State).

85 See, Black, The Canal and the Caribbean, in: R. Millett and W. Will (eds.), supra., note 80, at pp. 90—102. See also, Berner, The Panama Canal and Future United States Hemisphere Policy, (1980): Year Book of World Affairs, at pp. 205—219, and, Rubin, The Panama Canal Treaties: Locks on the Barn Door, (1981): Year Book of World Affairs, at pp. 181—193.

86 See, Plank, The United States and Cuba: Co-operation, Co-existence or Conflict, in: R. Millett and W. Will (eds.), supra., note 80, p. 117, at p. 119.

87 On Soviet interests in the Caribbean see, e.g., Duncan, Soviet and Cuban Interests in the Caribbean, in: id., at pp. 132—148. See also, J. Theberge (ed.), Russia in the Caribbean (Centre for Strategic and International Studies, Georgetown University, Washington, D.C.: 1973).

best interests to seek assistance from a country such as Cuba to forestall such an attack. We would view with displeasure any tendency on the part of Grenada to develop closer ties with Cuba."[88]
Thereafter the administration continued to apply pressure "in an attempt to force changes in the PRG's domestic policies and foreign relations".[89]

In October of 1979, following the "discovery" of a Soviet combat brigade in Cuba, relations between Washington and Havana deteriorated and American concern about the security of the Caribbean was reinforced. In an effort to contain Soviet and Cuban influence in the region the President announced a number of measures including the establishment of a permanent Caribbean Joint Task Force headquarters in Florida and the expansion of military exercises.[90]

If the attitude of the Carter administration to the PRG could be characterized as cool that of President Reagan was to prove to be positively hostile. As with his predecessor, the new President viewed the Caribbean as "a vital strategic and commercial artery for the United States".[91] Developments within the region were, however, from the start examined by his administration almost exclusively in terms of east-west ideological confrontation. As a recent British House of Commons report was to conclude, "the present Administration has a paranoid antagonism towards any government in the area which may be remotely described as left wing let alone Marxist".[92]

In his speech of 24 February 1982 to the Organization of American States in Washington D.C., in which he unveiled his much vaunted Caribbean Basin Initiative, President Reagan expressed anxiety over "the tightening grip of the totalitarian left in Grenada ...".[93] To Washington the perceived influence of Cuba on Grenada's development strategy and foreign policy was also a basis for concern. Security implications were seen to arise from the provision of Cuban assistance in military, security and allied spheres. These concerns were particularly acute in relation to the construction of a new international airport on the island. In a written submission of Decem-

---

88 Quoted by Gonsalves, supra., note 49, at p. 9.

89 Supra., note 54, at p. 46. See also, C. Searle, Grenada: The Struggle Against Destabilization (Writers and Readers etc. Ltd., London: 1983).

90 See, text of the address to the nation by President Carter of 1 Oct. 1979 (text provided by U.S. Dept. of State). See also, supra., note 54, at p. 32.

91 See, e.g., text of address by President Reagan to the Organization of American States on 24 Feb. 1982. Reproduced in: Current Policy, No. 370 (U.S. Dept. of State).

92 Supra., note 15, at para. 190.

93 Supra., note 91.

ber 1981 to a subcommittee of the Senate Foreign Relations Committee the State Department opined:

"The planned 9,800-foot Port Salines runway . . . has clear military potential. Such an airfield will allow operations of every aircraft in the Soviet/ Cuban inventory. Cuba's MiG aircraft and troop transports will enjoy a greater radius of operation. The airport will give Cuba a guaranteed refuelling stop for military flights to Africa."[94]

To show its displeasure with PRG policy it sought to isolate Grenada to the extent possible. It was, for instance, barred from the benefits of aid programmes such as the Caribbean Basin Initiative.[95] Pressure was also put on America's allies, and international institutions, to take similar steps though with mixed results.[96] Reagan also refused to accept the credentials of Grenada's Ambassador to the United States and ordered the American Ambassador in Barbados not to present his letters of credence in St. George's, the Grenada capital.[97]

As part of a more general effort to discourage communist expansion in the region the United States government continued to mount frequent military exercises. Indeed, in early 1982 it staged three significant military shows of strength in the Caribbean within a period of eight weeks.[98] One such exercise was mounted off Puerto Rico in October 1981. Under the code-name "Amber and the Amberines" the participating units rehearsed procedures for the removal of an unfriendly island government and the temporary occupation of state territory pending elections.[99] It is not surprising that "[t]his US navy manoeuvre in the northern Caribbean was seen by the PRG as a rehearsal for an attack on Grenada and the Grenadines".[100]

94 Reproduced in: supra., note 15, at p. 322.
95 This U.S. policy was formally opposed by CARICOM. See, e.g., Communiqué: Fourth Meeting of the Conference of Heads of Government of the Caribbean Community, supra., note 61, at p. 31.
96 See, e.g., supra., note 54, at p. 46; and, supra., note 57, at p. 167.
97 See, 'The Times' (London), 13 March, 1982.
98 See, 'The Guardian' (London), 24 April, 1982.
99 See, supra., note 57, at p. 167.
100 Supra., note 15, at para. 116.

5. The Anatomy of the Grenada Intervention

As the final quarter of 1983 approached, the political situation in the eastern Caribbean nonetheless appeared stable. The PRG continued to exercise effective control within Grenada and there was no coherent opposition to it within or without the island state. At the regional level there were growing signs that, notwithstanding concern over PRG attitudes and policies, the concept of ideological pluralism was taking root within CARICOM.[101] Furthermore, the membership of that organization continued to affirm a commitment to the peaceful settlement of disputes and opposition to the use of force for the solution of international controversies.[102] At the international level the critical attitude displayed by the PRG towards the destruction by the Soviet Union of a Korean commercial airliner was but one indication of a possible loosening of ties with the eastern block.

To all outward appearances the position of Prime Minister Bishop, a popular and charismatic leader, was secure. This appeared to be confirmed by his decision to undertake a week long tour of eastern European capitals, followed by two days of talks in early October with Cuban officials on his way home.[103] It is now known, however, that there was a significant degree of dissatisfaction with his leadership within the Central Committee of the ruling New Jewel Movement.

On the night of 13 October this division within the ruling group resulted in the placing of Prime Minister Bishop under house arrest. This became public knowledge on the following day and immediately provoked specula-

101 The 13 point Ocho Rios Declaration adopted at the 3rd Meeting of the CARICOM Heads of Government in 1982 included the following wording: "(4) Assert that while recognising the emergence of ideological pluralism in the Community responds to internal processes and is an irreversible trend within the international system, we are committed to ensuring that it will not inhibit the processes of integration." (1982) 16: Caribbean Monthly Bulletin, No's. 11—12, p. 31, at p. 32.

102 See, id., at points (7) — (9). At the 4th Meeting of the CARICOM Heads of Government in July 1983 it was stated that: "The Conference deplored the increasing resort to violence as a means of resolving conflicts and disputes between States. It called on all States to abstain from all forms of aggression and to use dialogue and negotiation to settle those conflicts which now threaten the peace and security of the Region." (1983) 9: Bulletin of Eastern Caribbean Affairs, No. 3, p. 27, at p. 28.

103 See, supra., note 38, at p. 3.

tion that Deputy Prime Minister Coard was the likely instigator and potential beneficiary of the leadership change.[104]

Discussions concerning the course of events in Grenada within the Reagan administration appear to have commenced even before Bishop's arrest, and by 14 October the State Department had initiated a review of the standard evacuation plan for Grenada. "The Office of the Joint Chiefs of Staff was asked to review contingency evacuation plans."[105]

Disquiet over the Grenada situation spread swiftly throughout the Commonwealth Caribbean and was compounded on 15 October by the announcement of the arrest of a number of other Cabinet Ministers. On the same day Prime Minister Adams of Barbados "sought opinion" on the possibility of effecting the rescue of Bishop from his captors.[106] Also on that day, it has been reported, an official of the Barbados Ministry of Defence and Security was "tentatively approached by a United States official about the prospect of rescuing Maurice Bishop from his captors and had been made an offer of transport".[107]

Discussions within the U.S. executive branch continued on a daily basis in an interagency framework. The prime consideration was later stated to have been the safety of the substantial number of U.S. citizens, perhaps 1,000 persons, living on Grenada. This concern was intimated to the new authorities on the island on 18 October when the U.S. Embassy in Barbados issued "a formal request for assurances of their well-being".[108] These assurances were forthcoming on 19 October in the Grenadian response. That response was, however, considered to be inadequate and serious planning for a "non-permissive evacuation" was commenced.[109] In subsequent testimony before the House Armed Services Committee of the U.S. Congress Assistant Secretary of State Motley characterized the Grenadian diplomatic note in these words: "This answer contained no assurances, no concrete measures to safeguard foreign residents, just a bland assertion and a blunt slamming of the door."[110] American worries were not lessened by

---

104 See, Appendix No. 11. See also, 'Newsweek', 31 October, 1983 and 'The Bajan and South Caribbean', November 1983.

105 Prepared statement of Assistant Secretary of State for Inter American Affairs, Langhorne A. Motley before the House Armed Services Committee, 24 January, 1984 (typescript provided by U.S. Congress).

106 See, Appendix No. 11.

107 Id.

108 Supra., note 105.

109 See, id.

110 Id. On that day U.S. Ambassador Bish warned the State Department that:

a refusal to permit the U.S. Embassy plane to land in Grenada on the same day.

Disquiet grew to alarm within the Commonwealth Caribbean with the resignation of a number of members of Bishop's Cabinet including Foreign Minister Whiteman. An emergency meeting of the Barbados Cabinet was convened on 19 October at which it "was agreed to proceed with a rescue plan, in collaboration with Eastern Caribbean countries and larger non-Caribbean countries with the resources necessary to carry out such an intricate operation".[111]

While the Cabinet meeting in Bridgetown was still in progress news was received that a crowd of Grenadians, led by Whiteman, had rescued the Prime Minister from house arrest. This group then proceeded in the direction of the capital seemingly with the intent of freeing other detained Ministers. Troops from the People's Revolutionary Army intervened and shot into the crowd causing a significant number of civilian casualties. Bishop, along with three former Cabinet colleagues and two trade union leaders, was reportedly arrested by the armed forces and immediately executed.[112] The formation of a Revolutionary Military Council (RMC) headed by General Hudson Austin was announced and a round-the-clock, shoot-on-sight 96 hour curfew imposed.[113]

The reaction to these events in the Caribbean was one of genuine revulsion and outrage. Political condemnation followed swiftly. On the following day, 20 October, the Government of Trinidad and Tobago unilaterally imposed a series of diplomatic, travel and economic sanctions on Grenada.[114] On the same day the Prime Minister of St. Lucia sought

"There appears to be imminent danger to U.S. citizens resident on Grenada due to the current deteriorating situation ... Amembassy Bridgetown recommends that the United States should now be prepared to conduct an emergency evacuation of U.S. citizens residing in Grenada." Id.

111 Appendix No. 11.

112 See, e.g., 'The Economist', 29 October, 1983 and 'The Guardian' (London), 21 October, 1983.

113 See, e.g., Appendix No. 9.

114 The following decisions were implemented with immediate effect: "Trinidad and Tobago would not participate in any CARICOM meetings whatsoever in which Grenada would be present; No Grenada citizens or nationals would be allowed entry into Trinidad and Tobago without a visa; No exports from Grenada into Trinidad and Tobago would be afforded CARICOM treatment and that no vessels registered in Grenada would be allowed the facilities of the CARICOM Jetty in Trinidad and Tobago." Statement by the Prime Minister of Trinidad and Tobago to the Trinidad Parliament, 26 October, 1983 (typescript provided by the High Commission of the Republic of Trinidad and Tobago, London).

support from certain of his Caribbean neighbours for a military solution.[115] The United States ordered the diversion of a naval and military force, *en route* to the Lebanon, towards Grenada.[116]

On Friday 21 October the Heads of Government of the members of the OECS, other than Grenada, gathered in Barbados. Following their meeting it was announced that it had been unanimously decided to impose immediate diplomatic and economic sanctions against the military regime.[117] It is now clear, although it was not then made public, that it was determined at the same meeting to remove the Revolutionary Military Council by force of arms.[118] In this context it was decided "to seek the assistance of friendly countries to stabilise the situation and to establish a peacekeeping force".[119] Barbados, which had been invited to attend the OECS meeting, immediately agreed. As Prime Minister Adams was later to report, "[t]roop numbers were settled and the staff of the Regional Security Organisation of which Barbados and most of the Eastern Caribbean States are members were deputed to do the necessary military planning".[120] It should be noted that St. Kitts/Nevis, which had only recently acquired full independence, though not a member of this security grouping, made arrangements to contribute a contingent. Montserrat, still a United Kingdom colony, was not in a position to take part though the action was supported by its political establishment.[121] Indeed, while permitting Montserrat to become a member of the OECS the United Kingdom had, pursuant to Article 23 of the treaty, notified "the intention of the Colony of Montserrat to withhold its participation in respect of Foreign Affairs and Defence and Security matters of the Organisation, to the extent that any decisions of the Organisation or any committee or institution thereof may require action to be taken by the Government of Montserrat inconsistent with

115 Appendix No. 11. Prime Minister Adams has noted that "later that day the Cabinet of Barbados decided to support a multi-national Intervention in Grenada after Caribbean Leaders had had an opportunity of discussing the situation and of jointly initiating action". Id.

116 See, supra., note 105. See also, 'Barbados Advocate' (Bridgetown), 22 October, 1983 (hereafter 'Barbados Advocate').

117 See, Appendix No. 5.

118 See, e.g., Appendix No. 9. Public speculation along these lines was, however, widespread. See, e.g., 'Barbados Advocate', 22 October, 1983.

119 Appendix No. 11.

120 Id. For extracts from the text of the treaty establishing this Regional Security grouping see, Appendix No. 4.

121 See, Appendix No. 14.

the views, directives, policies and obligations of Her Majesty's Government of the United Kingdom".[122]

Later that evening the Prime Ministers of Barbados and Dominica met Prime Minister Seaga of Jamaica, who had severed diplomatic relations with Grenada earlier in the week, and secured the participation of his country.[123] Finally, the United States Ambassador was informed of the decisions which had been taken and was issued an invitation for American participation.[124] Consequently U.S. military planning "shifted into a multilateral mode".[125]

On Saturday, 22 October, an emergency meeting of CARICOM Heads of Government took place in Port-of-Spain, Trinidad which continued into 23 October. Yet again Grenada, though a CARICOM member, was not permitted to participate. Following a lengthy debate the decision was taken by a majority of 11 to 1, the Guyana government being opposed, to impose a series of economic and diplomatic sanctions of a somewhat similar, though geographically more wide ranging, nature to those earlier agreed to at the sub-regional level.[126] The legal validity of such a majority decision in the face of a seemingly clear treaty requirement of unanimity must, however, be open to serious doubt.[127] No political consensus over the exercise of a military option emerged at this meeting. It is now known that, in addition to Guyana, Trinidad, Belize and the Bahamas were not in favour of intervention through force of arms.[128]

In Grenada, meanwhile, the curfew which had been imposed by the RMC had proved to be effective and had been lifted for a short period to allow for food purchases and similar activities.[129] On 22 October permission was given for the visit of two U.S. diplomatic representatives to the island. According to recent testimony before the U.S. Congress, these officials concluded that "the potential for violence even greater than that

---

122 Appendix No. 3.
123 See, Appendix No. 11. The formal written letter of invitation to Jamaica was communicated, along with enclosures, under date of 23 October and is reproduced within Appendix No. 10.
124 See, Appendix No. 11.
125 Supra., note 105.
126 These are detailed in the statement of the Prime Minister of Trinidad, supra., note 114. See also, 'Bardados Advocate', 24 October 1983.
127 See, e.g., Dundas, The Law of the Caribbean Community — A Statement, supra., note 61, at pp. 18—19.
128 See, e.g., supra., note 114.
129 See, 'Barbados Advocate', 22 October, 1983.

of October 19 was high, with concomitant risk to U.S. citizens".[130] Interestingly, these U.S. diplomats were accompanied by the United Kingdom Deputy High Commissioner in Barbados who was charged with making a first-hand assessment of the plight of British citizens.[131] It appears that he concluded that military action was not warranted in the circumstances.[132] Upon his return to Barbados this British official was reported to have informed the press that: "The situation in Grenada, with a 24-hour curfew which so far as I could see was virtually 100 per cent observed, is calm, tense and pretty volatile."[133]

Also during that weekend the RMC received reports, which were to prove to be extremely accurate, that plans were being formulated for a military intervention. As a result a diplomatic note, dated 23 October, was delivered to the American authorities. Having first expressed the view that any invasion would be "a rude violation of Grenada's sovereignty and of international law", the note went on to address itself to the position of foreign nationals. It reads in part thus:

"We reiterate that the lives, well-being and property of every American and other foreign citizens residing in Grenada are fully protected and guaranteed by our government. However, any American or foreign citizen in our country who desires to leave Grenada for whatever reasons can fully do so using the normal procedures through our airports on commercial aircraft. As far as we are concerned, these aircraft can be regular flights or chartered flights and we will facilitate them in every way we can."[134]

In addition, Radio Free Grenada broadcast, on Sunday night, a series of announcements warning of an impending invasion and calling upon the local militia to report for duty.[135]

One other event originating in Grenada during this period must be mentioned though it is still, to an extent, shrouded in mystery. It has been asserted that the Governor-General of Grenada, Sir Paul Scoon, was contacted through the offices of a non-participating state in connection with this intervention plan. In the words of Prime Minister Adams: "His opinion

---

130 Supra., note 105.

131 See, House of Commons, Parliamentary Debates, 26. October, 1983, col. 300.

132 See, id., at col. 301 and col. 332.

133 'Barbados Advocate', 24 October 1983.

134 Appendix No. 6. It appears that subsequently a number of efforts were made to bring out citizens of various nationalities by states other than the U.S. and with mixed results.

135 See, 'Barbados Advocate', 24 October 1983.

and approval were obtained, and arrangements made for him to issue a formal invitation as soon as it was physically safe for him to do so."[136] Subsequently, the text of a letter from the Governor-General to the Barbados Prime Minister, dated 24 October, was produced which embodied such an invitation.[137]

Following final Presidential approval on the evening of 24 October the military action was put into operation. Using the vast resources and fire-power of a U.S. carrier task force stationed off the Grenada coast, and with airborne backup from forces using the international airport on Barbados, military landings were effected on Tuesday, 25 October. Resistance by troops loyal to the RMC, assisted by a substantial number of Cuban "construction workers", was more intense than had been anticipated. Nonetheless, by 28 October all of the major military objectives of the intervening multinational force had been secured.[138]

The member states of the OECS voted on 29 October to remove the sanctions which had previously been imposed on Grenada.[139] Final pockets of resistance were quelled by 3 November. The Governor-General was invited to form an interim-administration to pave the way for a return to democracy, expected to take place in late 1984. By mid-December 1983 the vast majority of the American armed forces had been withdrawn leaving the maintenance of internal security to the Caribbean forces which had participated in the removal of the RMC and the local police.

From my limited vantage point in Barbados at the time of these events, reinforced by subsequent visits to St. Lucia and Trinidad and press reports, it was apparent to me that this military action was warmly welcomed by the majority of the people of the Commonwealth Caribbean. From such evidence as has come to light since, the people of Grenada appear to have viewed the situation in much the same light. Whether this action was justifiable in international law, irrespective of the views of the people of the region, is the subject to which the study now turns.[140]

136 Appendix No. 14.
137 See, Appendix No. 7. For the date see, supra., note 105. Efforts were made to obtain the text of this letter from he office of the Barbadian Prime Minister, but no reply was received.
138 See, e.g., 'Time', 7 November, 1983; 'Newsweek', 14 November, 1983; and, 'Maclean's', 7 November, 1983.
139 See, Appendix No. 12.
140 For an interesting perspective on the value of such an inquiry see the editorial entitled "Legal Problems" in the 'Barbados Advocate', 2 November, 1983.

PART II
THE GRENADA INTERVENTION IN INTERNATIONAL LAW

1. Justifications and Reactions

With the landing of the multinational force on Grenada the participating governments moved swiftly to justify their actions and to seek diplomatic support. At the political and moral level all were to point to the unsavoury nature of the group which had come to power and the brutal methods to which they had resorted. The OECS expressed, for example, on 25 October, 1983 its deep concern "that there would be further loss of life, personal injury and a general deterioration of public order as the military group in control attempted to secure its position".[1] The RMC was variously described as "a gang of murderers"[2], "men of the most brutal type"[3] and "a brutal group of leftist thugs"[4].

At the level of public international law three broad grounds were advanced as legitimizing the use of force. Firstly, all participating nations asserted that this military initiative was lawfully undertaken pursuant to the authority of Article 8 of the treaty establishing the OECS.[5] Secondly, the United States emphasized that its actions were also justified by the need to protect its nationals residing in Grenada.[6] Thirdly, all of the states in question asserted that the use of force was validated by a prior invitation issued by the Governor-General, Grenada's Head of State.[7]

1 Appendix No. 9.
2 The words of Prime Minister Adams. Appendix No. 11.
3 The words of Prime Minister Seaga. Appendix No. 10.
4 The words of President Reagan in a White House address on 25 October 1983 (text provided by the U.S. Embassy, Barbados).
5 See, Pt. II, (2) (b) infra.
6 See, Pt. II, (2) (c) infra.
7 See, Pt. II, (2) (d) infra.

The reaction of the international community as a whole was not, however, supportive of the intervention or impressed by the justifications offered for it. Within the Commonwealth Caribbean the government of Trinidad and Tobago expressed regret that force had been resorted to.[8] As Prime Minister Chambers was to remark on 26 October:

"Last year the Heads of Government of CARICOM, at their meeting in Ocho Rios, took specific decisions against the use of force in the resolution of disputes. More recently, in July of this year at the fourth conference of Heads of Government of CARICOM countries in Port of Spain, they reiterated this commitment to the non-use of force. The Government of Trinidad and Tobago, as a party to these decisions, could not now depart from these agreed principles particularly without resort in the first instance to efforts at a peaceful resolution of the problem."[9]

On the same day the government of Guyana, in unequivocal language, condemned the "invasion" as contrary to international law and a violation of the U.N. Charter.[10]

Outwith the Caribbean the reaction to the intervention was virtually unanimously hostile. Even the United Kingdom Government of Margaret Thatcher, normally most understanding of President Reagan's foreign policy, and with close and historic ties of friendship with the Commonwealth states involved, made it clear that it "took the view that no such action was called for".[11] The absence of diplomatic support for the participants became even more evident when the issue was debated in the United Nations. A draft Security Council resolution, proposed by Guyana and Nicaragua[12], which was forthright in condemning the action, failed only because of the use of the veto power by the United States.[13] Subsequently, the General Assembly, by a substantial majority[14], deeply deplored "the armed intervention in Grenada, which constitutes a flagrant violation of international law and of the independence, sovereignty and territorial integrity of that State".[15]

8 See, supra., Pt. I, note 114.

9 Id.

10 See, Press Release No. 20/83, dated 27 Oct. 1983, of the Guyana High Commission, London. See also, 'Caribbean Contact' (Bridgetown, Barbados), Dec. 1983.

11 The words of the U.K. Foreign Secretary to the House of Commons on 26 Oct. 1983, supra., Pt. I, note 131.

12 For the text see, Appendix No. 8.

13 The vote was 11 in favour, 1 against, 3 abstentions.

14 The vote was 108 in favour, 9 against, and 27 abstentions.

15 Appendix No. 13.

It is the purpose of the remainder of this preliminary analysis to determine whether or not this characterization of the action by the General Assembly can be said to be firmly based in contemporary international law.

2. The Grenada Intervention in International Law

a) Introduction

As is well known, the imposition of significant restraints on the right of states to resort to armed force for the solution of international controversies is of relatively recent origin. In the nineteenth century the liberty of states to wage war was regarded as inherent in the concept of sovereignty.[16] At the same time, international law did, curiously enough, seek to regulate the use of force short of war. Such a state of affairs was clearly unsatisfactory.[17]

It is not surprising that, in the light of the horror and carnage of the 1914–1918 war, efforts should have been made to circumscribe this traditional freedom which states had enjoyed. In this the Covenant of the League of Nations was a major landmark. Although the Covenant did not seek to abolish war, its provisions, particularly Articles 12 to 16, did significantly limit, for League members, the instances in which recourse to war would be legitimate.[18] As Brierly has noted, the relevant provisions of the text "made it very improbable that an aggression-minded state would ever succeed in resorting to war without a breach of its obligations under the Covenant".[19]

The League system was, however, generally regarded as deficient in a number of respects. The lack of universality of League membership weakened the effectiveness of the new approach and gaps remained in the

16 See, e.g., J. Brierly, The Law of Nations (Clarendon Press, Oxford: 6th ed. 1963), at pp. 397–398.

17 See, e.g., G. Schwarzenberger, A Manual of International Law (Professional Books Ltd., Abingdon: 6th ed. 1976), at p. 149.

18 See, e.g., the memorandum of 17 March, 1929, prepared for the U.K. Cabinet by the Foreign Secretary. Public Record Office, London, CAB 24/202, CP 85(29). For basic information on the functions and powers of the League see, e.g., L. Oppenheim, International Law (Longmans, Green & Co., London: 8th ed. 1955), at pp. 380–399.

19 Supra., note 16, at p. 408.

prohibition on recourse to war itself.[20] For these reasons several efforts were made, mainly in the 1920's, to improve upon the Covenant.[21] Of these the most significant was the 1928 Pact of Paris. Under its provisions the numerous contracting powers condemned "recourse to war for the solution of international controversies", and renounced it "as an instrument of national policy in their relations with one another".[22]

These and other initiatives in the inter-war period not only, arguably, resulted in a transformation of the previous customary rule[23] but also provided a sound basis on which the Charter of the United Nations could build. The general approach adopted by the framers of the Charter "to save succeeding generations from the scourge of war ..." can be briefly stated.[24] Firstly, states are obligated to "settle their international disputes by peaceful means in such a manner that international peace and security, and justice, are not endangered".[25] Secondly, in Article 2(4), often described as the "corner stone" of the Charter system, member states agree to a broad prohibition on the use of force. It reads:

"All Members shall refrain in their international relations from the threat or use of force against the territorial integrity or political independence of any State, or in any other manner inconsistent with the Purposes of the United Nations."[26]

The above prohibition of the threat or use of force is in turn made subject to a number of express limitations. Specifically excepted from the reach of Article 2(4) are actions taken or authorized by the United Nations

20 See, e.g., F. Hinsley, Power and the Pursuit of Peace (Cambridge University Press, Cambridge: 1963), at pp. 309—322. For a good history of the League see generally, F. Walters, A History of the League of Nations (Oxford University Press, London: 1952).

21 See, e.g., Essential Facts About the League of Nations (League of Nations, Geneva: 6th revised ed. 1936), at pp. 108—117.

22 Cmd. 3410 (1929).

23 See, e.g., I. Brownlie, International Law and the Use of Force by States (Clarendon Press, Oxford: 1963), at pp. 107—111.

24 Wording as used in the Preamble to the UN Charter.

25 Art. 2(3). See also, Arts. 10—14, 33—38 and 97—101. See generally, Bowett, The United Nations and Peaceful Settlement, in: International Disputes: The Legal Aspects (David Davies Memorial Institute of International Studies, London: 1972), at pp. 179—209.

26 In drafting this provision the word "war" was deliberately omitted. See, e.g., L. Goodrich, E. Hambro and A. Simons, Charter of the United Nations (Columbia University Press, London: 3rd revised ed. 1966), at pp. 43—50.

in certain circumstances[27]; the use of force in individual or collective self-defence[28]; military action against former enemy states[29]; and, certain actions taken by regional arrangements or agencies[30].

This scheme is, on the face of it, fairly straightforward. Indeed, Professor Rostow has recently remarked that, "[s]ince the Charter of the United Nations was drafted and ratified in 1945, the nominal law on the international use of force has been clear — as law goes, remarkably clear. Its essential terms can be summarized more easily (and with less real controversy) than most branches of the law of tort or contract".[31] Were this in fact the case, it would be a relatively easy task, given sufficient factual data, objectively to assess the legality of any use of force at the international level. Unfortunately, as we shall now see, such a view neglects the widespread doctrinal controversies which surround many central aspects of the Charter regime. These stem, in the main, from the ambiguities of wording found in the textual provision in question; ambiguities which states have, in practice, sought to exploit to their own advantage.

b) Article 8 of the OECS Treaty

As was noted earlier, all of the states which participated in the October 1983 military intervention in Grenada sought to justify such action, in part, by reference to Article 8 of the 1981 treaty establishing the OECS. That being said, subsequent elaborations of this ground indicate a divergence of legal analysis between the United States government on the one hand and the Commonwealth Caribbean governments on the other.

Emphasis was placed on Article 8 from the outset by U.S. officials. For instance, rather cryptic reference was made to the OECS treaty by President Reagan, in the presence of Prime Minister Charles of Dominica, at their joint press briefing at the White House on the morning of 25 October.[32] Later that day Secretary of State Shultz went some way towards clarifying the American position. He noted that the United States had received an

27 See, Ch. VII of the Charter.
28 See, Art. 51 of the Charter.
29 See, Arts. 53 and 107 of the Charter.
30 See, Ch. VIII of the Charter.
31 Rostow, The Politics of Force, in: (1982) Year Book of World Affairs, p. 38, at p. 58.
32 See, supra., note 4.

urgent request from the OECS, joined by Barbados and Jamaica, "to help them in their desire to ensure peace and stability in their area", and that "their analysis of the situation, in terms of the atmosphere of violent uncertainty, paralleled our own".[33] He then stated that "in response to the request of this organisation and in line with a request that they made pursuant to Article VIII of their treaty, bringing them ... together, the President decided to respond to their request ...".[34]

On 27 October U.S. Ambassador Kirkpatrick informed the UN Security Council that the collective action so undertaken "fully comported with relevant provisions of the UN Charter, which accord regional organizations the authority to undertake collective action".[35] On the same day Deputy Secretary of State Dam, in testimony before the Senate Foreign Relations Committee, made clear that his government viewed the collective action as being fully justified by the provisions of Chapter VIII of the Charter concerning regional arrangements.[36] On 4 November Deputy Secretary Dam, in an address in Louisville, remarked:

"... the OECS determined to take action under the 1981 treaty establishing that Organization. That treaty contains a number of provisions ... which deal with local as well as external threats to peace and security. Both the OAS Charter, in Articles 22 and 28, and the UN Charter, in Article 52, recognize the competence of regional security bodies in ensuring regional peace and stability. Article 22 of the OAS Charter in particular makes clear that action pursuant to a special security treaty in force does not constitute intervention or use of force otherwise prohibited by Articles 18 or 20 of that Charter. In taking lawful collective action, the OECS countries were entitled to call upon friendly states for appropriate assistance, and it was lawful for the United States, Jamaica and Barbados to respond to this request."[37]

By way of contrast, the language of justification used by the Commonwealth Caribbean states has been more evocative of collective action in self-defence pursuant to Article 51 of the UN Charter. Thus, in the annex to the 23 October OECS letter of invitation to Jamaica, the background to

---

33 25 Oct. 1983 Press Conference given by Secretary of State Shultz (transcript provided by the U.S. Embassy, Barbados).

34 Id.

35 Taken from the excerpts reproduced in: supra., Pt. I, note 38, p. 12, at p. 13.

36 Taken from the excerpts reproduced in: id., at p. 16.

37 Address to the Associated Press Managing Editors Conference, Louisville, Kentucky (transcript provided by the U.S. Embassy, Barbados).

the then situation in Grenada as viewed by its membership having been noted in some detail, it is stated that:

"Under the authority of Article 8 of the treaty ... the Authority proposes to take action for collective defence and the preservation of peace and security against external aggression by requesting assistance from friendly countries to provide transport, logistics support and additional military personnel to assist the efforts of the O.E.C.S. to stabilize this most grave situation within the Eastern Caribbean." [38]

In its Press Release of 25 October the OECS stated that three governments had responded to the request "to form a multi-national force for the purpose of undertaking a pre-emptive defensive strike in order to remove this dangerous threat to the peace and security of their sub-region and to establish a situation of normality in Grenada".[39] Somewhat similar wording was employed by the Prime Minister of Jamaica on the same day.[40]

A number of serious difficulties surround the Article 8 argument whether framed in terms of collective action under Chapter VIII of the Charter or as collective self-defence under Article 51 thereof.

The initial problem which such justifications encounter is to be found in the text of the 1981 treaty itself. Firstly, Article 8, which deals with the composition and functions of the OECS Defence and Security Committee, does not appear to authorize or envisage coercive military action against any member state. By virtue of section 3 it "shall advise the Authority on matters relating to external defence and on arrangements for collective security against external aggression, including mercenary aggression, with or without the support of internal or national elements".[41] This emphasis on external aggression is further reflected in section 4, where the same committee is charged with the co-ordination of efforts and development of ties among members "in matters of external defence and security ... in the exercise of the inherent right of individual or collective self-defense recognised by Article 51 of the Charter of the United Nations".[42]

That concerted action against a member state was not contemplated by the drafters of the treaty is reinforced by other provisions of the text. For example, under Article 3, the member states undertake to promote the purposes and functions of the organisation in the sphere of mutual defence

38 Reproduced in Appendix No. 10.

39 Appendix No. 9.

40 See, Appendix No. 10.

41 Appendix No. 2.

42 Id.

and security by endeavouring to "harmonise and pursue joint policies[43]; language hardly evocative of Chapter VII of the UN Charter. Furthermore, and following a regional practice established by CARICOM, the decisions of both the Defence and Security Committee[44] and the Authority of Heads of Government[45] are specifically required to be unanimous.

At the extraordinary session of the OECS Authority[46], held in Barbados on 21 October, at which the decision was taken to initiate military action and impose sanctions, Grenada was not represented. It appears, moreover, that the RMC was not invited to attend and would have been prevented from doing so had it so wished. Indeed, one of the sanctions agreed to at the meeting was that "the regime would not be permitted to participate in the deliberations of the organisation".[47]

It is clear, therefore, that the strict unanimity requirement was not met on 21 October. It might be argued, however, that the decisions there taken were *intra vires* the powers of the organisation on the ground that, given what amounted to the suspension of Grenada, they had been determined by all parties properly entitled to vote at that time. Such an argument, however, required that one imply a power of suspension in a text which makes express provision only for voluntary withdrawal.[48] Perhaps more plausibly, it might be argued that the subsequent invitation issued by Govenor-General Scoon for the military intervention to take place had the effect of validating at least those decisions which related directly to that course of action. Such an argument might be seen to find some force in the wording of Article 6(5) of the treaty. It reads in relevant part:

"All such decisions shall require the affirmative vote of all Member States present and voting at the meeting of the Authority at which such decisions shall have no force and effect until ratified by those Member States, if any, which were not present at that meeting, or until such Member States have notified the Authority of their decision to abstain."

The complex issues surrounding the status, if any, to be accorded to the Governor-General's request is the subject of detailed review later in this analysis. Suffice it for present purposes to note that Article 6 of the OECS

43 Id.
44 See, id., Art. 8(5).
45 See, id., Art. 6(5).
46 As authorized by Art. 6(11), id.
47 Appendix No. 5.
48 See, Appendix No. 2, Art. 24.

treaty establishes that "[t]he Authority shall be composed of Heads of Government of the Member States"[49] not of Heads of State.

Leaving to one side, for the present, the issue of the consent of Sir Paul Scoon and presuming, for the sake of argument, that the 21 October decisions of the Authority were *intra vires* the powers of the Organisation[50], a number of problems nonetheless remain.

Firstly, let us examine the contention of the United States that the military action taken pursuant to Article 8 was compatible with the provisions of Chapter VIII of the UN Charter.

As is well known, at the San Francisco Conference the states of Latin America insisted on the incorporation of provisions which would afford what they saw as due recognition to the importance of regional institutions.[51] These states were generally dissatisfied with the then prevailing conception of the universal organ as superior and regional organizations as subordinate instrumentalities for the maintenance of international peace and security. As Akehurst has noted:

"As small powers the Latin Americans were jealous of great power dominance in the Security Council, and were determined to delete the requirement that enforcement action under regional arrangements should be subject to authorization by the Security Council, which, they claimed, would enable an extra-regional great power to veto regional action and generally to interfere with regional affairs. After a prolonged deadlock, a compromise was finally reached with the insertion of Article 51 in the Charter, which would enable States, including regional groupings of States, to act in collective self-defence without Security Council authorization."[52]

Having thus secured the removal of the veto from collective action in self-defence, agreement was reached on the provisions which would establish the relationship between regional bodies and the UN. This agreement finds reflection in Articles 52 to 54 of the Charter, being Chapter VIII thereof.

---

49 Id., Art. 6(1).

50 As required by Art. 5(2), id.

51 See, e.g., Wood, The Organisation of American States, in: (1979) Year Book of World Affairs, p. 148, at pp. 150—151. See also, Akindele, The Organization of African Unity and the United Nations, in: (1971) Canadian Yearbook of International Law, p. 30, at pp. 30—33.

52 Akehurst, Enforcement Action by Regional Agencies with Special Reference to the Organization of American States, in: (1967) British Year Book of International Law, p. 175, at p. 176. See also, Kourula, infra., note 62, at p. 98 and p. 100.

It should be noted that the Charter nowhere defines regional arrangements or agencies. Such minimal conditions as may properly be regarded as set by Article 52[53] would, without much doubt, be satisfied by the OECS. Nonetheless, within the present context difficulty does arise for the American view that the Grenada intervention can be justified under the terms of Chapter VIII rather than by virtue of collective self-defence. This is so because of the wording of Article 53. It reads, in relevant part, as follows:

"1. The Security Council shall, where appropriate, utilize such regional arrangements or agencies for enforcement action under its authority. But no enforcement action shall be taken under regional arrangements without the authorization of the Security Council...".

On the face of it one might be tempted to suggest that the situation was clear: military action undertaken by a regional arrangement or agency, otherwise than in the exercise of the right of collective self-defence, required the prior authorization of the Security Council; an authorization which was neither sought nor obtained in this instance.

However, since 1945 the United States has, particularly within the context of the Organization of American States, sought to place a far more extensive interpretation on the powers of regional agencies.[54] To this end they have attempted to limit to an absolute minimum the activities which should be regarded as covered by the term "enforcement action" in Article 53. In this, the Americans have been assisted by the Advisory Opinion of the International Court of Justice in the *Expenses Case*.[55] That Opinion illustrates that there are an extensive range of activities of a collective nature, including peace-keeping operations, which cannot be said to constitute enforcement action.[56] There can be little doubt, however, that a non-permissive collective military intervention must constitute enforcement action if that phrase is not to lose all meaning. Indeed, in the *Expenses Case* the Court determined that the UN peace-keeping forces there in issue did not fall within the meaning of enforcement action, as used in the Charter, on the ground that they operated with the consent of the host states.[57]

53 See, e.g., Akehurst, id., at pp. 177—180. See also, Franck, Who Killed Article 2(4)? in: (1970) 64: American Journal of International Law, p. 809, at p. 832.

54 See, e.g., Franck, id., at p. 824.

55 1962 I.C.J. Reports, p. 151.

56 See, e.g., Pharand, Analysis of the Opinion of the International Court of Justice on Certain Expenses of the United Nations, in: (1963) Canadian Yearbook of International Law, p. 272 et seq.

The United States has also advanced in the past, particularly at the time of the Cuban missile crisis of 1962, a number of arguments intended to maximize the freedom of action of regional arrangements even when the use of force was contemplated without host state consent.[58] The thesis has been advanced, for example, that enforcement action, within the meaning of the Charter, refers to binding measures and therefore does not apply to actions taken pursuant to mere recommendations. As Akehurst, among others, has noted such reasoning finds little support in the *Expenses Case* where the "distinction between enforcement action and peace-keeping action was not based on the distinction between a decision and a recommendation, but on the presence or absence of consent by the States concerned".[59] In any event, in this case, such a form of argument is not available for use as the decisions of the OECS Authority are "binding on all Member States ...".[60]

It has also been argued that the authorization of the Security Council can be given both *post facto* and by implication. The view as to the latter is, in essence, that the failure of the Security Council to condemn an action of this type is tantamount to acquiescence, and, therefore, to implied authorization. In the case of Grenada, as noted earlier, the failure of the

---

57 The Court stated, in part, that "the operations of ONUC did not include a use of armed force against a State which the Security Council, under Article 39, determined to have committed an act of aggression or to have breached the peace. The armed forces which were utilized in the Congo were not authorized to take military action against any State. The operation did not involve 'preventative or enforcement measures' against any State under Chapter VII and therefore did not constitute 'action' as that term is used in Article 11." Supra., note 55. On the central role of host state consent as a basis for UN peace-keeping action see generally, Garvey, United Nations Peace-keeping and Host State Consent, in: (1970) 64: American Journal of International Law, pp. 241—269, and Di Blase, The Role of the Host State's Consent with Regard to Non-Coercive Actions by the United Nations, in: A. Cassese (ed.), United Nations Peace-Keeping: Legal Essays (Sijthoff & Noordhoff, Alphen aan den Rijn: 1978), at pp. 55—94. See also, Higgins, A General Assessment of United Nations Peace-Keeping, in: A. Cassese (ed.), id., p. 1, at pp. 4—7. For an indication that the view of the I.C.J. may have constituted a liberal interpretation of the intended meaning of "enforcement action" as used in the Charter see, e.g., supra., note 26, at pp. 365—367.

58 See, e.g., Chayes, The Legal Case for U.S. Action on Cuba, in: (1962) 47: United States Department of State Bulletin, p. 763 et seq., and Meeker, Defensive Quarantine and the Law, in: (1963) 57: American Journal of International Law, p. 515 et seq.

59 Supra., note 52, at p. 202.

60 Appendix No. 2, Art. 6 (5).

Security Council to condemn resulted only from the exercise of the American veto power.

Although Schwebel has suggested that "[t]here is ample room for difference of view on the validity of these constructions"[61], the majority of scholars have rejected such theories as unsound.[62] In the view of the present writer such arguments fall clearly outwith the penumbra of uncertainty surrounding the meaning of Article 53. They are at best politically self-serving, and legally spurious, attempts to justify otherwise illicit uses of military might. In short, save with the validly expressed consent of the relevant Grenadian authorities, an issue to be examined at a later stage, an argument which seeks justification in Chapter VIII of the Charter must fail.

The view that the military action in Grenada was taken in a legitimate exercise of the right of collective self-defence is not open to objections of the same kind. Consent by the state affected by the exercise of that right has never been deemed a requirement, and such action is not subject to the prior authorization of the Security Council. Indeed, an argument based on collective self-defence, if warranted by the circumstances of this case, would be arguably valid even if the decisions taken by the OECS were deemed to be *ultra vires* the organisation for want of unanimity or other reasons. This would be so since no institutional structure is required for the proper exercise of the right. The question which must be addressed therefore is whether or not the circumstances of the Grenada crisis gave rise to a valid exercise of collective defensive action.

The right of states to use armed force in self-defence has for long been recognized in international law. The circumstances in which a plea of self-defence would be regarded as legitimate crystallized in the modern state system of the 19th century and were not altered by either the Covenant of the League of Nations or by the 1928 Pact of Paris.[63]

---

61 Schwebel, Aggression, Intervention and Self-Defence in Modern International Law, in: (1972) 136: Hague Recueil, p. 419, at p. 477.

62 See, e.g., supra., note 52, at pp. 216—219; Farer, Limiting Intraregional Violence, in: T. Farer (ed.), The Future of the Inter-American System (Praeger Publishers, London: 1979), p. 195, at p. 200; Akindele, supra., note 51, at pp. 34—35; R. Churchill and A. Lowe, The Law of the Sea (Manchester University Press, Manchester: 1983), at p. 153; and, Kourula, Peace-Keeping and Regional Arrangements, in A. Cassese (ed.), op. cit., at pp. 107—108 and pp. 115—118.

63 For the view of the U.K. as to the latter see, e.g., D. Harris, Cases and Materials on International Law (Sweet and Maxwell, London: 3rd ed. 1983), at pp. 640—641.

Unlike the Covenant and the Pact, however, the subject of self-defence was the subject of specific treatment in the UN Charter. Article 51 reads: *"Nothing in the present Charter shall impair the inherent right of individual or collective self-defence if an armed attack occurs against a Member of the United Nations, until the Security Council has taken measures necessary to maintain international peace and security. Measures taken by members in the exercise of this right of self-defence shall be immediately reported to the Security Council and shall not in any way affect the authority and responsibility of the Security Council under the present Charter to take at any time such action as it deems necessary in order to maintain or restore international peace and security."*

As was noted earlier, the decision to make explicit mention of self-defence in the text was taken primarily for the purpose of clarifying the position in regard to its collective exercise by regional arrangements and agencies rather than by a desire to alter the circumstances traditionally associated with its legitimate exercise.[64]

For this reason the conditions which govern this strictly limited right are to be found in the pre-Charter rules of customary international law. There is substantial evidence to suggest that the formulation of the conditions as to its exercise which was agreed by the United States and the United Kingdom in diplomatic correspondence arising out of the *Caroline* incident of 1837 accurately reflect the position in customary law.[65] In the oft quoted note from U.S. Secretary of State Webster to the British Minister to Washington of 24 April 1841 it was stated that:

'It will be for [Her Majesty's] Government to show a necessity of self-defence, instant, overwhelming, leaving no choice of means, and no moment for deliberation. It will be for it to show, also, that the local authorities of Canada — even supposing the necessity of the moment authorized them to enter the territories of the United States at all — did nothing unreasonable or excessive; since the act justified by the necessity of self-defence, must be limited by that necessity, and kept clearly within it . . .".[66]

---

64 For the U.K. view to this effect see, Cmd. 6666 (1945), at p. 9. See also, statement of the Lord Chancellor on 1 Nov., 1956, Parl. Deb. H.L., Vol. 199, cols. 1348—1359.

65 See, e.g., supra., note 16, at pp. 403—408, and Behuniak, The Seizure and Recovery of the S.S. Mayaguez, in: (1979) 83: Military Law Review, p. 59, at pp. 73—75. But see, supra., note 23, at pp. 258—261.

66 Lord McNair, International Law Opinions (Cambridge University Press, Cambridge: 1956), Vol. II, p. 222.

In the British Government's reply of 28 July 1842 agreement was expressed with the above formulation although it was then contended, on the facts, that the incident fell within its scope.[67] At the conclusion of the second world war the Nuremberg Tribunal "expressly endorsed the statement of Secretary Webster in the *Caroline* as to the proper limits of the right ...".[68] This and other evidence concerning the customary rule, extensively treated elsewhere[69], reveals three central concerns; necessity[70]; proportionality[71]; and its protective or preventative, rather than punitive, purpose[72].

Notwithstanding the wealth of authority concerning the nature and extent of the right of self-defence in customary law, considerable difficulties have arisen as to its proper exercise in the Charter era. Of particular importance in the present context is the controversy surrounding the validity of anticipatory self-defence. Here the central question is whether or not Article 51 of the Charter requires a state to await an actual armed strike against its territory before resorting to the use of force.

A considerable body of opinion denies that any such right exists.[73] This school of thought stresses the use of the words "if an armed attack occurs" in Article 51 and argues that this means that the armed attack must have occurred before force can be validly used in self-defence. These, and other arguments of a legal nature, are said to find support in a number of prac-

---

67 See, id., at pp. 222—223.

68 Supra., note 16, at pp. 406—407. See, Cmd. 6964 (1946), at p. 28.

69 See, e.g., B. Cheng, General Principles of Law (Stevens & Sons Ltd., London: 1953), at pp. 92—97.

70 See, e.g., The Sloop Ralph 39 U.S. Court of Claims, p. 204, at p. 207. In addition to posing an "instant" danger there should be "no choice of means". As Cheng has remarked, supra., note 69, at p. 95: "It is not a case of necessary or legitimate self-defence if the danger can be averted by such lawful means as admonition, protest or diplomatic representation."

71 A report made to the League of Nations in 1927 said: "Legitimate defence implies the adoption of measures proportionate to the seriousness of the attack and justified by the seriousness of the danger." Quoted in: supra., note 63, at p. 657. See also, The Blodgett Case, 12 Metcalf, p. 56, at p. 84.

72 See, supra., note 69, at pp. 94—95, and supra., note 16, at p. 421.

73 See, e.g., supra., note 23, at pp. 275—278; M. Akehurst, A Modern Introduction to International Law (George Allen and Unwin, London: 4th ed. 1982), at pp. 222—223; Skubiszewski, Use of Force by States. Collective Security. Law of War and Neutrality, in: M. Sørensen (ed.), Manual of Public International Law (Macmillan, London: 1968), p. 739, at p. 767; and, Henkin, Force, Intervention and Neutrality in Contemporary International Law, in: (1963) Proceedings of the American Society of International Law, p. 147, at p. 150.

tical and policy considerations.[74] Should this narrow view of the reach of legitimate self-defence under the Charter be regarded as valid, then any argument advanced along these lines to justify the Grenada intervention must fail for want of a prior armed attack by the forces of that state against the territory of any other country. The question of whether an armed attack against nationals would suffice is reviewed in detail at a later stage of this study.

In opposition to this narrow, or "sitting duck", theory there are those who argue that anticipatory action may legitimately be resorted to. In essence, scholars and governments espousing this approach rely on the opening words of Article 51; viz., "Nothing in the present Charter shall impair the inherent right of individual or collective self-defence ...". This wording, it is said, demonstrates an intention not to alter (impair) the pre-existing (inherent) customary rule.[75] As Bowett, a noted adherent of this view, has stated, "the whole purpose of Article 51 ... was to preserve the traditional right".[76] It is further asserted that such an anticipatory right formed part of customary law as affirmed by the International Military Tribunal for the Far East when addressing the legality of the invasion of certain Dutch colonial territory by Japan during the second world war.[77] This school of thought has also marshalled a number of subsidiary legal arguments and asserts that their approach is supported by a variety of extra-legal considerations.[78]

This broader view of the scope of the right of self-defence under the UN Charter is, without doubt, more favourable to the position of those countries which participated in the October 1983 Grenada intervention. For that reason, and for purposes of argument only, the circumstances of that military action will now be reviewed on the assumption that anticipatory self-defence may still be regarded as legitimate. It will also be

---

74 See, e.g., supra., note 23, at pp. 257—261.

75 The attachment of the U.K. government to the "inherent" nature of self-defence was stressed throughout the recent Falkland Islands conflict. See, e.g., The Falkland Islands: The Facts (H.M.S.O., London: 1982), at pp. 11—12.

76 Bowett, The Interrelation of Theories of Intervention and Self-Defence, in: J. Moore (ed.), Law and Civil War in the Modern World (Johns Hopkins University Press, Baltimore: 1974), p. 38, at pp. 39—40.

77 Quoted in: supra., note 63, at pp. 656—657. See also, M. Whiteman, Digest of International Law (U.S. Govt. Printing Office, Washington, D.C.: 1971), Vol. 12, at pp. 47—48.

78 Some of the defects of this approach are noted by Franck, supra., note 53, at pp. 820—822.

assumed, for these purposes, that if the situation was one in which action in self-defence was justified, all of the participating states in question were entitled to exercise such a right collectively.[79]

On this basis it is sufficient to examine whether the circumstances prevailing in Grenada were such as to fall within the exacting criteria laid down in the *Caroline* case. In the first instance, therefore, one must demonstrate "a necessity of self-defence, instant, overwhelming, leaving no choice of means and no moment for deliberation". The perception of the OECS states as to the nature of the threat posed to their security by the situation in Grenada can be determined, in part, from the text of the enclosure to their official invitation of 23 October to the government of Jamaica to participate in the military action.[80] A number of points are there advanced to justify resort to arms "for collective defence and the preservation of peace and security against external aggression ...". Firstly, it is asserted that the overthrow of the Bishop administration "took place with the knowledge and connivance of forces unfriendly to the O.E.C.S. ...". No further elaboration of this ground is offered. In this case it must, however, be assumed to relate to the possible role of Cuba in these events. Suffice it to say for present purposes that no substantial evidence has come to my attention to suggest that the Cuban authorities were directly involved in bringing about the removal of Prime Minister Bishop from power or his subsequent execution. Indeed, such a view is incompatible with the official Cuban reaction to those events (if taken at face value), which was, to say the least, negative in character.[81] It may also be of interest to note that no mention was made of this factor in the subsequent OECS statement on Grenada dated 25 October.[82] Nor, for that matter, is it alluded to in the letter of invitation from Governor-General Scoon to the Prime Minister of Barbados calling for military intervention.[83] In any event, such involvement by a foreign power, even if it did take place, would not seem to be sufficient, in and of itself, to bring the Grenada situation within the ambit of the *Caroline* rule.

79 For one view which argues in favour of a limited right to join in collective action of this type see, Bowett, Collective Self-Defence Under the Charter of the United Nations, in: (1955—56) 32: British Year Book of International Law, pp. 130—161. For an instance of the contrary approach see, e.g., supra., note 23, at pp. 328—333.

80 Reproduced within Appendix No. 10.

81 For the full text of the Cuban statement see, 'Barbados Advocate', 22 Oct. 1983. See also, 'Newsweek', 31 Oct. 1983.

82 See, Appendix No. 9.

83 See, Appendix No. 7.

The 23 October OECS annex also noted "the current anarchical conditions, the serious violations of human rights and bloodshed that have occured, and the consequent unprecedented threat to the peace and security of the region created by the vacuum of authority in Grenada".[84] This, and similar formulations[85], can be said to relate largely to the position of foreign nationals and other civilians within Grenada and will be addressed separately, and in some detail, at a later stage of this study. For present purposes one might note that there is evidence to suggest, as we have seen, that although the RMC was not well received by the inhabitants of Grenada its actions in the few days on which it was in power do not rest easily with a suggested "vacuum of authority" within the state. In particular, its most significant exercise of authority, the imposition of a rather draconian curfew, seems to have been substantially complied with. It might also be argued that there is no self-evident nexus between a "vacuum of authority" and the anticipation of an armed attack against the territory of a third state.

On 23 October the OECS also drew the attention of the government of Jamaica to the deep concern felt over the existing and possible future strength of Grenada's military forces, against which its members had no effective means of defence.[86] On 25 October the OECS again articulated this view:

"Member Governments are ... greatly concerned that the extensive military build up in Grenada over the last few years had created a situation of disproportionate military strength between Grenada and other OECS countries. This military might in the hands of the present group posed a serious threat to the security of the OECS countries and other neighbouring States."[87]

Shortly after the military intervention had taken place, the OECS drew attention to "the extensive quantity of military equipment discovered in Grenada by the multinational force" and characterized this "as further evidence in support of their earlier claims of the serious threat posed to the peace and security of the sub-region involving foreign elements".[88]

---

84 Appendix No. 10.

85 In his letter of 24 Oct. the Governor-General stated: "You are aware that there is a vacuum of authority in Grenada following the killing of the Prime Minister and the subsequent serious violations of human rights and bloodshed." Appendix No. 7.

86 Appendix No. 10.

87 Appendix No. 9.

88 Appendix No. 12. The reference to "foreign elements" is seemingly to the source

A number of difficulties are raised by arguments of this type. Firstly, there is no credible evidence, of which I am aware, to suggest that the armed forces of Grenada were actively preparing for an armed incursion into the territory of any Caribbean state.[89] Secondly, it has not been demonstrated how an island state with no air or naval force at its command could actually undertake such a military initiative. The intended assistance of a third state or states in any such venture cannot be assumed and has not been proved. Thirdly, the arms used by Grenadian forces in resisting the military intervention, and those subsequently discovered to have been stockpiled, were overwhelmingly of a type normally characterized as defensive in nature.[90] At perhaps a more serious level, it is not difficult to conceive of the problems which would arise at the international level if it were to be accepted that the mere possession by a state of an armed force significantly superior to that of its neighbours was sufficient to trigger the exercise of an anticipatory right of self-defence.

In this context it would also be necessary to demonstrate that there were no other lawful means of protection available for use by the participating states. In the words of Secretary of State Webster, there should be "no choice of means and no moment for deliberation". It is not, therefore, an instance of legitimate self-defence if the danger could be averted by such peaceful means as diplomatic representation, protest or the imposition of economic and similar sanctions.[91]

As has been seen, it was the view of the government of Trinidad and Tobago that it could not sanction the use of force "without resort in the first instance to efforts at a peaceful resolution of the problem".[92] Indeed, such a course of action was urged upon the United States in the 23 October diplomatic note from the RMC.[93]

It is, of course, correct to say that the government of Trinidad and the

of the large quantities of arms found by the multinational force. See, e.g., supra., Pt. I, note 38, at p. 16. See also, Grenada: A Preliminary Report (U.S. Department of State and Department of Defense, Washington, D.C.: 16 Dec. 1983), at pp. 27–30.

89 Any such intention was disavowed in the Grenada diplomatic note of 23 Oct. 1983 where it is stated that: "Grenada has not and is not threatening the use of force against any country and we do not have such aspirations." Appendix No. 6.

90 See, references at note 88, supra.

91 See, note 70, supra.

92 Supra., Pt. I, note 114.

93 See, Appendix No. 6.

OECS had sought a resolution of the Grenada problem through the prior imposition of economic, diplomatic and other sanctions, and that a somewhat similar strategy had been agreed to by the emergency meeting of the CARICOM Heads of Government. It should, however, be noted that the first of these initiatives had been in effect for less than a week before the military intervention took place. Furthermore, as detailed above, although the OECS agreed to impose sanctions on Grenada at its 21 October emergency meeting, it also decided at that time to remove the RMC by force of arms. Given the seeming absence of an immediate military threat to any of its members, it would be difficult to fashion a convincing argument that non-military initiatives had had sufficient time to bring about the desired resolution of the Grenada problem. Indeed, the public OECS decision to impose sanctions might appear to some to have been a mere cloak for the then private determination to resort to force rather than a genuine effort to seek a peaceful resolution of the crisis.

In conclusion, it is not easy to see how the situation prevailing in Grenada during October 1983 could be properly characterized as posing a threat to the security of neighbouring states such as to justify, within the meaning of international law, the use of force in anticipation of an armed attack. This conclusion appears to this writer to be so self-evident, on the facts presently available, as not to call for an examination of the additional criteria which would have to be met to legitimize any actual use of force in self-defence. In particular, it is not deemed necessary to address the difficult question of whether or not the level of force actually resorted to on 25 October by the multinational force was "proportionate to the threat, as required by international law".[94]

c) Intervention for the Protection of Nationals

Although all of the states which contributed to the multinational military intervention of 25 October expressed concern over the reported violations of basic human rights in Grenada, including the execution of political leaders and the murder of innocent civilians by troops loyal to the RMC,

94 Supra., note 75, at p. 12. See also, Zafren, 'The Intervention in Grenada' (Congressional Research Service, Library of Congress, Washington, D.C.: typescript dated 27 Oct. 1983), p. CRS—8: "It must satisfactorily be shown that in a given situation not only was there a legal right to intervene but that the operation of that intervention was carried out according to the dictates of international law."

only the government of the United States was to emphasize intervention for the protection of its nationals as a central justification for its actions.

The need to act "to protect innocent lives, including up to 1,000 Americans", was stated by President Reagan to have been one of the three reasons for U.S. participation.[95] Similarly, Secretary of State Shultz noted on 25 October that the United States had joined in the collective action, in part, "to secure the safety of American citizens . . . and, for that matter, the citizens of other countries . . . and to assure that any who wish to leave may do so".[96] Both the President[97] and the Secretary of State[98] made it clear, however, that the decision to act was taken in this context in order to prevent U.S. nationals from coming to harm and not because of any actual acts or threats directed against such persons. Similar arguments were advanced by the U.S. in the UN Security Council on 27 October.[99] On 4 November U.S. Deputy Secretary of State Dam detailed the American position in these words:

". . . U.S. action to secure and evacuate endangered U.S. citizens on the island was undertaken in accordance with well-established principles of international law regarding the protection of one's nationals . . . There is absolutely no requirement of international law that compelled the United States to await further deterioration of the situation that would have jeopardized a successful operation. Nor was the United States required to await actual violence against U.S. citizens before rescuing them from the anarchic and threatening conditions . . .".[100]

There can be no doubt that intervention, in the sense of a "dictatorial interference by a State in the affairs of another State for the purpose of maintaining or altering the actual condition of things"[101] is, as a general rule, prohibited by international law.[102] Nor can it be doubted that the

---

95 Supra., note 4.

96 Supra., note 33.

97 The President said: "This was a case of not waiting until something actually happened to them." Supra., note 4.

98 The Secretary of State said: "He [the President] felt that it is better under the circumstances to act before they might be hurt or be hostage than to take any chance, given the great uncertainty clearly present in the situation." Supra., note 33.

99 See, supra., note 35, at p. 13.

100 Supra., note 37.

101 L. Oppenheim, supra., note 18, at p. 305.

102 See, e.g., Waldock, The Regulation of the Use of Force by Individual States in International Law, in: (1952) II: Hague Recueil, at p. 467.

landing of armed forces in the territory of a third state, without its consent, is, *prima facie*, intervention. That being said, and leaving for subsequent consideration the question of possible prior consent in this instance, it is necessary to examine the issue of whether international law recognizes the protection of nationals as an exception to this prohibition.

In spite of the fact that the pre-Covenant customary law seems to have recognized the right of states to intervene, in certain circumstances, for the protection of their nationals, the issue of whether this right survived into the Charter era is both contentious and confused. A number of scholars[103], and a majority of states[104], adopt a negative view. In essence the proponents of this analysis afford a broad interpretation to the prohibition on the threat or use of force contained in Article 2(4) of the UN Charter. To what they see as a general prohibition against the threat or use of force they admit only the exception of action in self-defence under Article 51. Some then define, as we have seen, the ambit of the self-defence exception as comprehending only those situations in which an armed attack against state territory has actually taken place. Others, such as Brownlie, deny that intervention of this nature was encompassed within the customary right of self-defence and cannot, therefore, be regarded as saved by Article 51 irrespective of its scope.[105] This "restrictionist theory" claims support in post-1945 state practice, in various resolutions of the UN General Assembly[106], and in the judgement of the International Court of Justice in the *Corfu Channel* case.[107]

The validity of the above view is contested by two distinct schools of thought. In the first of these, most commonly identified with a suggested right of humanitarian intervention unrelated to national status, an emphasis is placed on a restrictive interpretation of the reach of Article 2(4) of the Charter.[108] Under this approach it is suggested that a use of force which is

103 See, e.g., Skubiszewski, supra., note 73, at pp. 758—759; Akehurst, The Use of Force to Protect Nationals Abroad, in: (1977) 5: International Relations, p. 3, at p. 3 and pp. 16—17; and, supra., note 23, at pp. 298—301.

104 See, e.g., D'Angelo, Resort to Force by States to Protect Nationals, in: (1981) 21: Virginia Journal of International Law, p. 485, at p. 487; and, M. Akehurst, supra., note 73, at p. 224.

105 Supra., note 23, at pp. 298—301.

106 See, G.A. Res. 2131 (XX) and G.A. Res. 2625 (XXV).

107 I.C.J. Reports 1949, p. 4. See also, Akehurst, supra., note 103, at pp. 17—18. But see, supra., note 23, at pp. 288—289.

108 See, e.g., Fonteyne, The Doctrine of Humanitarian Intervention: Its Current Status Under the United Nations Charter, in: (1974) 4: California Western International Law Journal, at pp. 203—270.

not directed "against the territorial integrity or political independence" of a state and which is consistent with "the Purposes of the United Nations" is lawful.[109]

The second school of thought seeks to justify intervention on behalf of nationals on the basis that it is permitted by Article 51. As Bowett has stated, "[i]ntervention for the protection of the intervening states' own nationals traditionally has been and still is today a part of the customary right of self-defense".[110] This approach is grounded in the fact that at international law an injury to a national arising from an act or omission by a foreign state within its own territory is in law an injury to that individual's state of nationality.[111]

Interestingly, all three of the major post-war state proponents of the right of intervention on behalf of nationals have embraced the self-defence view. The United Kingdom, for example, sought to justify its participation in the Anglo-French invasion of Suez in 1956, in part, on this basis. The Lord Chancellor informed the House of Lords at the time that "self-defence undoubtedly includes a situation in which the lives of a State's nationals abroad are threatened and it is necessary to intervene on that territory for their protection ...".[112] Similarly, the government of Israel sought to base its 1976 incursion into the territory of Uganda in the so-called Entebbe incident on the same theory.[113] More importantly for present purposes, the United States has tended to justify many of its not infrequent military interventions in this way.[114] In recent years, for example, the U.S. has prof-

109 See, e.g., D'Angelo, supra., note 104, at pp. 491—498, and pp. 518—519; and, Jeffery, The American Hostages in Tehran, in: (1981) 30: International and Comparative Law Quarterly, at pp. 717—729. An argument along these lines was advanced by the U.K. agent before the ICJ in the Corfu Channel Case, but was not specifically treated by the Court in its judgement. See, supra., note 63, at p. 643. But see, Farer, The Regulation of Foreign Intervention in Civil Armed Conflict, in: (1974) 142: Hague Recueil, p. 297, at pp. 387—388.

110 Supra., note 76, at p. 44.

111 See, e.g., Head, A Fresh Look at the Local Remedies Rule, in: (1967) Canadian Yearbook of International Law, p. 142, at p. 147; W. Bishop, International Law (Little Brown & Co., Boston: 3rd ed.), at pp. 822—851; and, F. Garcia-Amador, L. Sohn and R. Baxter, Recent Codification of the Law of State Responsibility for injuries to Aliens (Oceana Publications, Dobbs Ferry: 1974), at pp. 143—164.

112 Supra., note 64. See also, M. Whiteman, supra., note 77, at p. 190.

113 This view was made clear by Ambassador Herzog in the Security Council. See, supra., note 63, at pp. 669—670. See also, Knisbacher, The Entebbe Operation: A Legal Analysis of Israel's Rescue Mission, in: (1977) 12: Journal of International Law and Economics, at pp. 57—83.

114 See, e.g., supra., note 23, at pp. 292—294; supra., note 102, at pp. 466—467.

fered a self-defence analysis both of the *Mayaguez* rescue of 1975[115] and the abortive 1980 mission by elements of its armed forces to rescue members of its diplomatic and consular staff held hostage at its Embassy in Tehran.[116]

Given this U.S. affinity for the self-defence basis for interventions of this nature, it would seem to be appropriate, for purposes of argument, to examine the circumstances of the Grenada action within that context. Such a form of analysis is also of benefit to the U.S. position in that, of the two schools of thought favouring military action on behalf of nationals, the limiting criteria attached to Article 51 based action are, arguably, the less demanding.[117] Again for the purposes of argument, the frequently repeated assertion by those favourably disposed to the self-defence theory that it encompasses anticipatory action will be accepted as a correct statement of the position in law.

Common to the approach of scholars and states adopting the self-defence theory is the view that the right is circumscribed by the principles enunciated by Secretary of State Webster in the *Caroline* incident. As one leading academic authority has stated, the exercise of this right "must be subject to the normal requirements of self-defence".[118] To Waldock, action taken on this basis must satisfy the following principles derived from Webster's formula:

"There must be (1) an imminent threat of injury to nationals, (2) a failure or inability on the part of the territorial sovereign to protect them and (3) measures of protection strictly confined to the object of protecting them against injury. Even under customary law only an absolute necessity could justify an intervention to protect nationals." [119]

An almost identical formulation of the above text was advanced by the

Such a justification was advanced in relation to the Dominican Republic in 1965. See, e.g., M. Whiteman, supra., note 77, at pp. 192—196. See also, N. Leech, C. Oliver and J. Sweeney, The International Legal System (Foundation Press, Mineola: 1973), at pp. 1225—1227. The U.S. has also advanced such arguments to justify support for other states undertaking interventions on this basis. In relation to the Entebbe raid see, supra., note 63, at pp. 670—671; and, Knisbacher, id., at p. 78.

115 See generally, Behuniak, supra., note 65.

116 See, e.g., D'Angelo, supra., note 104, at p. 512.

117 See generally, supra., note 108. See also, D'Angelo, op. cit., at pp. 496—498.

118 Supra., note 76, at p. 44. See also, supra., note 16, at p. 402, and pp. 427—428.

119 Supra., note 102, at p. 467. See also, Fitzmaurice, The General Principles of International Law, in: (1957) II: Hague Recueil, at p. 173.

United Kingdom at the time of the Suez crisis in 1956.[120] Similarly, during the debates in the Security Council on the Israeli action at Entebbe in 1976 the United States Ambassador noted "a well established right to use limited force for the protection of one's own nationals from an imminent threat of injury or death in a situation where the State in whose territory they are located is either unwilling or unable to protect them. The right, flowing from the right of self-defence, is limited to such use of force as is necessary and appropriate to protect threatened nationals from injury".[121]

The available information clearly indicates that the U.S. was concerned about the safety of its citizens in Grenada even before the execution of Prime Minister Bishop and his colleagues on 19 October. As we have seen, on the previous day the Americans had issued "a formal request for assurances of their well-being".[122] The Grenadian response, received on 19 October reads in part: "... the interests of U.S. citizens are in no way threatened by the present situation in Grenada which the Ministry [of External Affairs] hastens to point out is a purely internal matter".[123] As was noted above, the content of this note was not such as to convince the U.S. government that its nationals were in no danger, and on the same day the American Embassy in Barbados urged that an emergency evacuation be undertaken.[124] Subsequent events within the island, including violation of human rights, bloodshed and the imposition of the severest form of curfew, could only have increased U.S. anxiety.

On the weekend before the intervention members of the U.S. diplomatic service were able to visit Grenada. It has been revealed that these officials "unanimously assessed the position of those officials they were able to meet as obstructionist and unco-operative. No coherent government seemed to be functioning or even forming. Conversations of Embassy officers with American citizens indicated that more than 300 wished to leave the island. In short, the potential for violence even greater than that of October 19 was high, with concomitant risk to U.S. citizens. An evacuation, permissive or not, would have been fully justified".[125]

Although the internal situation in Grenada was obviously such as to cause concern, it was not of such a nature as to self-evidently justify the

120 1 Nov. 1956 statement by the Lord Chancellor, supra., note 64.

121 Quoted at supra, note 63, at p. 671.

122 See, supra., Pt. I, note 105.

123 Quoted in, id.

124 See, id.

125 Id.

use of force. It will be recalled, for instance, that the United Kingdom Deputy High Commissioner in Barbados visited Grenada at the same time as the two U.S. diplomats in question.[126] It will also be recalled that the U.K. government not only shares the same view as to the legal position under Article 51 of the Charter but is closely allied to the United States. Nonetheless a different conclusion was drawn from an analysis of the same factual situation. As the Secretary of State for Foreign and Commonwealth Affairs was to inform the House of Commons on 26 October 1983: *"Taking account of all the legal and practical considerations, and of the interests of our citizens and their safety in these circumstances, we came to a different conclusion, as I explained to the House. We would not dispute that a state has the right in international law to take appropriate action to safeguard the lives of its citizens where there has been a breakdown of law and order, nor that there is any provision in the charter of the United States (sic) that makes it unlawful to take such action. Those are the considerations that no doubt the United States and those acting with it must have had in mind. We took a different view of all the circumstances that apply in this case."*[127]

Such an appreciation by the U.K. government is, of course, no more conclusive as to the legitimacy of resort to arms in this instance than the differing conclusion arrived at by the United States. It does, however, serve to indicate that even among such like minded states the situation was not regarded as in any way clear-cut.

It should also be stressed that there is evidence to indicate that the internal situation on the island did not pose "an imminent threat of injury" to U.S. citizens. In particular, it should be noted that, so far as is known, no action was taken, or threatened, against any group of foreign nationals by the RMC. Nor does it appear, on the information presently available, that actual injury was inflicted on foreign residents at the hands of private parties. Furthermore, given the relative effectiveness of the curfew which had been imposed it might be thought that RMC would have been in a position to protect such persons had they come under threat from such private parties.

As the RMC had neither failed to afford protection to such persons prior to the intervention nor lost its ability to continue to do so, the sole justification for the intervention must rest on an actual or presumed un-

---

126 In addition, and unlike the U.S., the U.K. maintained a permanent diplomatic presence on the island.

127 Supra., Pt. I, note 131, at col. 332.

willingness to continue such protection into the future. Exactly such an argument was broached by the U.S. in the Security Council on 27 October. Ambassador Kirkpatrick stated, in part, that:

"The madmen responsible for the coup in Grenada did not put their captured adversaries on trial; they simply murdered them in cold blood. In these circumstances it was fully reasonable for the United States to conclude that these madmen might decide, at any moment, to hold hostage the 1,000 American citizens on that island." [128]

In addition, it was asserted that U.S. nationals "were denied the right of free exit" and that "[t]he airport was closed and entry by humanitarian organizations and others concerned with their welfare was prevented".[129]

On 27 October Deputy Secretary of State Dam informed the U.S. Senate Foreign Relations Committee that: "Although the RMC gave assurances that the airport would be opened on October 24 and foreigners allowed to depart, they then failed to fulfil that assurance." [130]

It would appear that this latter remark was intended to refer, in part, to the diplomatic note, dated 23 October, presented by the RMC to American authorities. This, as we have seen, contained assurances that the lives, well-being and property of American and other foreign nationals "are fully protected and guaranteed by our government".[131] This note further stipulated that "any American or foreign citizen in our country who desires to leave Grenada for whatever reasons can fully do so using the normal procedures through our airports on commercial aircraft. As far as we are concerned, these aircraft can be regular flights or chartered flights and we will facilitate them in every way we can".[132]

The above can be considered to constitute an express and concrete undertaking to the United States government, which offered to it a lawful means for the protection of the interests of its citizens. In this context it should be noted that among the sanctions imposed by the 21 October emergency meeting of the OECS Authority was the termination of "all sea and air communications links with Grenada until further notice".[133]

128 Supra., note 35, at p. 13.

129 Id.

130 Supra., note 36.

131 Appendix No. 6. There is no doubt that this note was received. See, supra., note 38, at p. 4. See also, 'Time', 7 Nov. 1983.

132 Id. Verbal discussions with representatives of the RMC took place at this time, and to the same effect, in the presence of a U.K. diplomat. See, Grenada: A Preliminary Report, supra., note 88, at p. 37. See also, 'Barbados Advocate', 24 Oct. 1983 and 25 Oct. 1983.

133 Appendix No. 5.

This sanction, which was not lifted until 29 October[134], effectively precluded the evacuation of foreign nationals by air save through the use of chartered flights.[135] It does not appear from the record that the United States government made any direct attempt to put the undertaking given to it by the RMC to the test by seeking permission for such flights to land for the purpose of facilitating an evacuation of its nationals. Nor would it seem to be appropriate, under the circumstances, for the U.S. to predict the outcome of such an initiative from any failure of similar efforts by third states to whom similar undertakings may well not have been given.[136]

Given the above, it must be open to serious doubt whether it can be said that there was either an imminent threat to U.S. nationals, or a failure, inability or unwillingness on the part of the RMC to protect them. However, even if the conclusion were to be reached, on the basis of more detailed information than is available to the present writer, that the position of U.S. nationals could properly be characterized in one of these ways it would still be for the United States to demonstrate that the measures of protection resorted to were strictly "confined to the object of protecting them against injury".[137]

In discussing this requirement for the legitimate exercise of the right, it is common to make reference to the concepts of proportionality[138] and the limited nature of the permissible objective[139]. In practice it is notorious-

---

134 Appendix No. 12.

135 It has been reported that the U.K. was unable to evacuate its nationals by air prior to the invasion because the regional air carrier (LIAT) was "not allowed to make flights even for humanitarian reasons". 'Nation' (Bridgetown, Barbados), 25 Oct. 1983 (special evening edition).

136 This would appear to be particularly important given the subsequent U.S. acceptance of the fact that the operational airport on Grenada was n o t closed on 24 October. On 16 Dec. 1983 the U.S. government noted: "In fact, although a few small planes were allowed to land and depart, the airport was not open for normal traffic." Grenada: A Preliminary Report, supra., note 88, p. 37. See also, 'The Times' (London), 22 Nov. 1983. Among the aircraft allowed to land and depart on that day was one belonging to the U.S. Embassy, which was allowed to take several U.S. nationals with it. See, 'Barbados Advocate', 25 Oct. 1983. Similarly, nationals of certain other eastern Caribbean states were reported to have taken advantage of the opening of the airport for this purpose. See, id. Furthermore, on the evening of 24 Oct. the Foreign Minister of Trinidad and Tobago announced that arrangements had been made to evacuate Trinidadian and Canadian nationals by air on 25 Oct. See, 'Nation', supra., note 135.

137 Supra., note 102, p. 467.

138 See, e.g., Supra., note 76, at p. 44.

139 See, e.g., D'Angelo, supra., note 104, at p. 501.

ly difficult to apply, in a satisfactory manner, the rather elastic notion of proportionality to any use of force situation. For this reason we shall act upon the assumption that the armed might brought to bear in the Grenada conflict accorded with this requirement. Even with such a concession, however, the American action does not fit easily within the ambit of the criterion that it be strictly confined to the necessity of extricating its citizens from danger. In this instance the United States, with its allies, effected a total military occupation of the state; removed the RMC from the seat of power; arrested and detained members of the RMC; oversaw the establishment of an interim-government; and, retained a substantial troop presence on the island for a number of weeks, after those nationals who wished to leave Grenada had been evacuated.

In the light of what had been said above there appears to be a substantial *prima facie* case for suggesting that the United States justification for acting in defence of its nationals, in these circumstances, was unsound in law.

d) Intervention by Invitation

The final substantive legal ground advanced by the participating states was that their actions were legitimized by virtue of an invitation issued to them by the Governor-General of Grenada, Sir Paul Scoon.

Although still the subject of some uncertainty, it appears that the Governor-General did not initiate the discussions among neighbouring countries of a possible military solution to Grenada's internal problems. It seems as if the initial decision to follow this path was taken by the OECS and other interested states and that the approval of Sir Paul Scoon was then sought, though not directly, by them.[140] As Prime Minister Adams of Barbados was to explain on 9 December 1983, "Government having been destroyed in Grenada itself the Governor-General became the Constitutional Authority in the island who could formally invite foreign countries to enter and restore order. His opinion and approval were obtained, and arrangements made for him to issue a formal invitation as soon as it was physically safe for him to do so".[141] This reference to his personal safety no doubt relates to the fact that such an invitation could not have been issued with the advance knowledge of the RMC. Indeed, it appears that

140 See, Appendix No. 11.
141 Appendix No. 14.

the RMC moved to place the Governor-General under house arrest prior to the military intervention.[142]

The formal written invitation for action by the multilateral force became available only after Sir Paul Scoon had been rescued from his captors in the course of the intervention. It is embodied in the text of a letter, under date of 24 October, addressed to the Prime Minister of Barbados. It reads, in part, as follows:

"You are aware that there is a vacuum of authority in Grenada following the killing of the Prime Minister and the subsequent serious violations of human rights and bloodshed.

I am therefore seriously concerned over the lack of internal security in Grenada. Consequently I am requesting your help to assist me in stabilizing this grave and dangerous situation. It is my desire that a peace-keeping force should be established in Grenada to facilitate a rapid return to peace and tranquility and also a return to democratic rule." [143]

This basis for resorting to the use of force in Grenada has been emphasized repeatedly by the U.S. government. For example, Deputy Secretary of State Dam has intimated that the United States "and the OECS countries accorded his appeal exceptional moral and legal weight. The invitation of lawful governmental authority constitutes a recognized basis under international law for foreign states to provide requested assistance".[144]

The action taken by Governor-General Scoon in inviting foreign military forces to intervene in the affairs of Grenada raises a number of difficult issues of constitutional and international law.[145] At the constitutional level these difficulties stem from the fact that the office of Governor-General in independent Commonwealth Caribbean states is not designed for the exercise of substantive governmental powers. It is intended, in the main, as a symbol of and a focal point for national unity. The essentially ceremonial role intended for the Governor-General is clearly evident in the 1973 independence constitution of Grenada. Although designated "Her Majesty's representative in Grenada"[146], the text of the constitution and the opera-

---

142 See, 'The Guardian' (London), 28 Oct. 1983.

143 Appendix No. 7.

144 Supra., note 37.

145 For some interesting contributions to the public debate on the constitutional question see, 'The Guardian' (London), 31 Oct. 1983; 'The Financial Times' (London), 31 Oct. 1983; and, 'The Weekend Nation' (Bridgetown, Barbados), 11 Nov. 1983.

146 The Grenada Constitution Order, SI No. 2155 (1973), s. 19.

tion of constitutional convention left the Governor-General without real power. For instance, in relation to the exercise of executive authority the 1973 constitution required him to "act in accordance with the advice of the Cabinet except in cases where he is required by this Constitution or any other law to act in accordance with the advice of any person or authority other than the Cabinet or in his own deliberate judgement".[147] Under this scheme, for example, the prerogative powers in the sphere of external affairs were properly exercisable only upon the advice of the responsible Minister.[148]

In only two important matters of government did the independence constitution leave to the Governor-General power to act in his discretion. The first of these related to the appointment of the Prime Minister[149] although his choice was circumscribed by a number of provisions including the requirement that he "appoint a member of the House of Representatives who appears to him likely to command the support of the majority of the members of the House".[150] The second related to the role of the Governor-General in the legislative process. In particular, by virtue of section 45(2): "When a bill is submitted to the Governor-General for assent in accordance with the provisions of this constitution he shall signify that he assents or that he withholds assent". The circumstances in which assent could properly be refused were, in turn, determined by well settled constitutional conventions. In addition, this seeming power of veto was in reality effectively nullified by the equally well settled conventional rule that the Queen will appoint or remove an individual from the office of Governor-General upon the advice of the Prime Minister of Grenada.[151]

Sir Paul Scoon was appointed to the office of Governor-General upon the advice of Sir Eric Gairy. When Gairy was overthrown in March 1979, he remained in office notwithstanding the fact that the change in government had taken place in violation of the terms of the 1973 constitution and that that instrument was then suspended.[152] Although the PRG determined that "[t]he Head of State shall remain Her Majesty the Queen

147 Id. s. 62(1).
148 As is the case elsewhere in the Commonwealth Caribbean monarchies. See, e.g., L. Barnett, The Constitutional Law of Jamaica (Oxford University Press, London: 1977), at p. 172.
149 See, supra., note 146, s. 58(1).
150 Id., s. 58(2).
151 As is generally the case elsewhere. See, e.g., supra., note 148, at p. 170.
152 Grenada People's Law No. 1. (1979).

and her representative in this country shall countinue to be the Governor-General ..."[153], he was simultaneously stripped of the few significant discretionary powers which he had previously enjoyed. In particular, it was declared that "all executive and legislative power" was vested in the PRG, which would also be responsible for the appointment of the Prime Minister.[154] As Alexis has remarked: "Only in Grenada is the Head of State not given even a formal role in the making of legislation. All legislative power is vested in the PRG, a body to which the Head of State does not belong."[155] The purely ceremonial nature of the position of Governor-General under the new order, in which he acquiesced, became clear when it was determined in March 1979 that he would be restricted to performing "such functions as the People's Revolutionary Government may from time to time advise".[156]

As there has been no suggestion that Sir Paul Scoon issued this invitation pursuant to the advice of the PRG it follows that such an action would normally be beyond his proper constitutional powers and hence of no effect in the internal law of Grenada. Whether under the post-1979 constitutional arrangements he could be said to possess a reserve power to act without advice in a crisis, and if so to what extent, is a matter of debate to which we now turn.

The first issue to be addressed in this context is the extent to which the crisis in Grenada of October 1983 was constitutional as well as political in nature. The constitutional question, in turn, must be seen to revolve around the process by which Prime Minister Bishop was removed from office. As was noted above, in the post-1979 constitutional order the Prime Minister was to be appointed by the PRG. There does not, however, appear to have been enacted a specific statutory provision governing the method by which he might be dismissed from office. In such circumstances Alexis would seem to have been correct in assuming that the agency responsible for his appointment could effect his removal.[157]

The present writer has been unable to determine whether the removal of the Prime Minister from post was effected by a decision of the PRG act-

153 Grenada People's Law No. 3. (1979).
154 Grenada People's Law No. 2. (1979).
155 F. Alexis, supra., Pt. I, note 43, at p. 58.
156 Grenada People's Law No. 3. (1979).
157 See, supra., Pt. I, note 43, at p. 93 and p. 111. Curiously for a Commonwealth Caribbean polity, the PRG, in turn, appointed its own members. See, id., at p. 58. See also, Grenada People's Law No. 12. (1979).

ing pursuant to its normal procedures.[158] If this were to prove to be the case, the resulting situation in Grenada could not be properly characterized as a constitutional crisis and no question of the exercise of a reserve power by the Governor-General would arise. On this basis the subsequent invitation to foreign military force would, without doubt, be unconstitutional.

For the purposes of the present analysis, and given the lack of sufficient factual data, it will be assumed that the change in leadership did not result from the operation of constitutionally proper processes. In such a situation it would seem possible to fashion a credible argument favouring the constitutionality of the action taken by Sir Paul Scoon. In this case his Ministers had been murdered, imprisoned or had resigned their offices. Consequently there was, in effect, no duly constituted authority capable of proffering the required advice. A vacuum of authority could then be said to exist in which, arguably, by force of necessity the Governor-General was capable of acting in his own deliberate judgement. Only on the basis of such a form of reasoning could the invitation issued by Sir Paul Scoon be regarded as valid in the context of Grenadian municipal law.[159]

It can, no doubt, be argued that international law is not in any event concerned with the intricacies of the internal law of any state and that other members of the international community are entitled to rely upon the ostensible authority of a Head of State. Such an argument would find support in the context of the law of treaties and in the available international jurisprudence.

Thus, the 1969 Vienna Convention on the Law of Treaties stipulates that Heads of State, Heads of Government and Ministers of Foreign Affairs are to be considered as representing their states for the purpose of all acts relating to the conclusion of a treaty without the need to produce full powers.[160] Similarly, pronouncements in the *Eastern Greenland*[161] and *Free Zones*[162] cases clearly indicate the reluctance of international adjudicative agencies to look behind the seeming authority of state agents.

---

158 For one analysis of the procedure followed and related circumstances see, Grenada: A Preliminary Report, supra., note 88, at pp. 31—35. For the text of the remarks of General Austin on 17 Oct. 1983 see, 'The Bajan and South Caribbean', Nov. 1983, at pp. 9—10.

159 Such a view finds support in the text of the letter of invitation issued by the Governor-General. See, Appendix No. 7.

160 Vienna Convention on the Law of Treaties, 1969, Article 7(2)(b). See also, (1966) II: Yearbook of the International Law Commission, at pp. 192—193.

161 PCIJ, Ser. A/B, No. 53, at pp. 56—71 and p. 91.

162 PCIJ, Ser. A/B, No. 46, at p. 170.

It should be noted, however, that the Vienna Convention does include, among the grounds of invalidity of treaties, the case in which an agreement is entered into in violation of provisions of internal law regarding competence to conclude treaties.[163] The decision to include this provision in the draft articles prepared for use by the Vienna Conference by the International Law Commission (ILC) was arrived at only with difficulty.

Three schools of thought on this issue were identified by the ILC. First, there were jurists who maintained "that constitutional laws governing the formation and expression of a State's consent to a treaty have always to be taken into account in considering whether an international act . . . is effective to bind the State".[164] Second, there were those scholars who argued that "good faith requires that only notorious constitutional limitations with which other States can reasonably be expected to acquaint themselves should be taken into account".[165] The final group of authorities held to the view that international law was not properly concerned with the internal constitutional arrangement of states and that failure to comply with such provisions does not affect the validity of a treaty at international law.[166] As the ILC noted, the adherents of this view can call upon the support of the rather limited state practice and judicial authority in this area.[167]

Although the third approach mentioned above must be regarded as the orthodox one, it is, arguably, subject to exceptions. As the commentary to Article 43 of the 1966 ILC draft notes:

"Some of these writers modify the stringency of the rule in cases where the other State is actually aware of the failure to comply with internal law or where the lack of constitutional authority is so manifest that the other State must be deemed to have been aware of it." [168]

The Commission considered, and the Conference subsequently agreed, that the basic principle should be that non-observance of a provision of internal law should not be considered to vitiate the consent given by the state at the international level. Certain members of the Commission, however, felt that:

". . . it would be admissible to allow an exception in cases where the viola-

---

163 Art. 46 thereof.
164 (1966) II: Yearbook of the International Law Commission, at p. 240.
165 Id.
166 See, id., at p. 241.
167 See, id., at p. 241 and the citations thereat.
168 Id.

*tion of the internal law regarding competence to enter into treaties was ab-
solutely manifest. They had in mind cases, such as have occurred in the
past, where a Head of State enters into a treaty on his own responsibility
in contravention of an unequivocal provision of the constitution. They did
not feel that to allow this exception would compromise the basic principle,
since the other State could not legitimately claim to have relied upon a
consent given in such circumstances. This view prevailed in the Commission.* "[169]

Article 46 of the Vienna Convention, therefore, provides for the invalidity
of a treaty concluded "in violation of a provision of . . . internal law regarding competence to conclude treaties" in circumstances where such violation
"was manifest and concerned a rule of its internal law of fundamental
importance".[170]

By analogical extension of the principles on which Article 46 is based
it would not seem unreasonable to suggest that a request of this type, issued
solely by a Governor-General of a Commonwealth Caribbean state acting
in his own deliberate judgement, could not be legitimately relied upon by
third parties. At the basis of such a contention would be the view that the
primarily ceremonial position of a Governor-General, and his inability to
act in most areas of state activity save upon the advice of Ministers, were
concepts of fundamental constitutional importance, which "would be objectively evident to any State conducting itself in the matter in accordance
with normal practice and in good faith".[171]

On the other hand two possible lines of argument might be thought to
be available to negative such an approach. Firstly, it might be said that, in
the unusual circumstances here in question, action taken by the Governor-
General in his own deliberate judgement was not manifestly in excess of
his constitutional authority. Secondly, it might be argued, with some con-
viction, that the principles which are at the root of Article 46 are unknown
to customary international law, that the Article itself constitutes an
attempt at "progressive development" of the law, and that their proper
operation is confined to the law of treaties and then only for the parties to
the Vienna Convention.[172]

---

169 Id., p. 242.
170 Art. 46(1).
171 As required by Art. 46(2).
172 See, e.g., Nahlik, The Grounds of Invalidity and Termination of Treaties, in:
     (1971) 65: American Journal of International Law, p. 736, at p. 740. The Vienna
     Convention entered into foce on 27 Jan. 1980.

For the purposes of argument the remainder of this analysis will be based on the assumption that third states are entitled to rely upon a request of this type emanating from the office of a Head of State. Even upon this assumption, however, serious difficulties still confront a reliance by the participants in the multinational force upon the invitation issued by Sir Paul Scoon.

Given the central place of consent in international law, it has for long been assumed that "if a government invites another State to act in a manner which would otherwise constitute a derogation from the rights of the former, the presence of consent negatives the possibility of wrong".[173] For example, there can be no doubt that a state may "consent to the entry of foreign forces on [its] territory, to the passage of foreign forces, to operations by foreign forces on [its] territory and to the union of the state with another state".[174]

For this reason it has often been asserted that a military intervention undertaken pursuant to an invitation from the lawfully established government purges the action of any taint of illegality. State practice both before and since 1945 reveals frequent examples of military interventions being justified on this basis.[175] The United States, for example, proffered such an argument as validating its actions in the Lebanon in 1958.[176] The Soviet Union used a similar line of reasoning for its military interventions in Hungary in 1956, Czechoslovakia in 1968 and Afghanistan in 1979.[177]

The proponents of this open-ended view of legitimacy of intervention by invitation do acknowledge that its exercise will often present certain

---

173 Lauterpacht, The Contemporary Practice of the United Kingdom in the Field of International Law — Survey and Comment, V in: (1958) 7: International and Comparative Law Quarterly, p. 92, at p. 103.

174 Supra., note 23, at p. 317.

175 See, e.g., R. Higgins, The Development of International Law Through the Political Organs of the United Nations (Oxford University Press, London: 1963), at pp. 210—212.

176 See, e.g., Wright, United States Intervention in the Lebanon, in: (1959) 53: American Journal of International Law, at pp. 112—125.

177 See, e.g., Wright, Intervention, 1956, in: (1957) 51: American Journal of International Law, at pp. 257—276; and, supra., note 63, at pp. 651—653. For an examination of Soviet views on intervention generally see, Butler, Soviet Attitudes Toward Intervention, in: J. Moore (ed.), supra., note 76, at pp. 380—398; and, Schwebel, The Brezhnev Doctrine Replaced and Peaceful Co-Existence Enacted, in: (1972) 66: American Journal of International Law, at pp. 816—819. See also, Schwenninger, The 1980s: New Doctrines of Intervention or New Norms of Nonintervention? in: (1981) 33: Rutgers Law Review, at pp. 423—434.

difficulties of a factual nature. As Fawcett has explained, "it is often hard to determine whether intervening forces have come at the invitation or with the consent of the lawful government, and whether, even in the case of treaty arrangements, consent has been freely given and is not rather the product of hidden influence or pressure by the intervening power, which will be often found at work in countries on the power frontier".[178] Notwithstanding the uncertainty which still surrounds the exact circumstances in which the present invitation came to be issued, we will assume for purposes of argument that it is not open to objections of this kind.

Perhaps a majority of modern writers, however, question the right of a government to seek, and a foreign state to provide, military assistance in a civil war at least in those cases where there is no evidence to suggest that the insurgents are benefiting from the assistance of a foreign power.[179] This view, in turn, finds support in the majority practice of the UN General Assembly. In its 1965 Declaration on the Inadmissibility of Intervention in the Domestic Affairs of States, which was adopted with no negative votes and only one abstention, the General Assembly declared that no state shall "interfere in civil strife in another state".[180] The sole abstaining state was the United Kingdom which is, however, on record as supporting the view of non-intervention in civil strife. Thus, in 1967 a U.K. spokesman informed a UN special committee that "... if a country was unfortunate enough to fall into a situation in which control of the country was divided between warring factions and if no outside interference had taken place, then any form of interference or any encouragement given to any party was prohibited by international law".[181] The same view of the law is expressed in General Assembly Resolution 2625 (XXV), which was adopted by consensus on 24 October, 1970.[182]

The above doctrinal dispute, as we have seen, revolves around differing

178 The words of Fawcett quoted by M. Whiteman, supra., note 77, at p. 47.

179 See, e.g., supra., note 76, at p. 42; R. Higgins, supra., note 175, at pp. 210—211; supra., note 176; and supra., note 173, at p. 103. But see, e.g., Potter, Legal Aspects of the Beirut Landing, in: (1958) 52: American Journal of International Law, p. 727, at p. 728. For a recent analysis of the U.S. position see, E. McDowell (ed.), Digest of United States Practice in International Law 1976 (U.S. Govt. Printing Office, Washington, D.C.: 1977), at pp. 3—7. See also, Farer, supra., note 109, at pp. 318—320.

180 UNGA Res. 2131 (XX).

181 Quoted in: supra., note 63, at p. 651.

182 On the nature and importance of this practice see, e.g., Farer, supra., note 109, at pp. 365—367; and, E. Aréchaga, International Law in the Past Third of a Century, in: (1978) 159: Hague Recueil, at pp. 111—116.

views as to the legitimacy of affording military assistance to a regime attempting to supress armed dissidence. It is apparent, however, that the situation prevailing in Grenada on 25 October 1983 was not of this type. There is no evidence to suggest that those loyal to the executed Prime Minister, or to the Governor-General, were resisting by force of arms the assumption of power by the RMC.

Furthermore, the available evidence would seem to indicate that the RMC was, through the instrumentalities of repression available to it, in effective control of the entire territory of the state within the meaning of international law. As Wright has noted in words thought applicable to the position of Governor-General Scoon: "There is a presumption ... that a government, even if generally recognized, cannot speak for the state if it is not in firm possession of the state's territory. In international law the *de facto* situation is presumed to overrule the *de jure* situation — *ex factis jus oritur*." [183]

It is submitted that the invitation for military intervention issued by Sir Paul Scoon on 24 October should properly be regarded as having emanated from an agent of the previous constitutional order, which had been successfully replaced by a military coup.[184] In these circumstances there is little evidence to suggest that foreign countries would be entitled to rely upon such an invitation as legitimizing their use of force. It is believed that Mendelson, in a letter to 'The Times' of 8 November 1983, stated the position with legal accuracy. He wrote, in the specific context of Grenada, in part as follows:

" *Modern international law does in fact permit military intervention by outside states in support of established governments in certain limited circumstances. It does not, however, permit such intervention in support of governments which have actually been overthrown by internal revolution or coup d'état if the successors are effectively operating as a government.*

This is irrespective of the constitutional credentials or political complexion of the overthrown or their overthrowers. In short, the emphasis is on effectiveness, rather than legitimacy." [185]

183 Supra., note 176, at p. 120. In responding to this invitation the U.S. specifically stated that he represented legitimate governmental authority. It was not, therefore, viewed as a situation where there was no government in the state. See, E. McDowell (ed.), supra., note 179.

184 For another, earlier example of such an action by France in relation to Gabon see, Farer, supra., note 109, at p. 333.

185 'The Times' (London), 10 Nov. 1983.

3) Conclusion

Although too short a time has elapsed since the landing of the multinational force on Grenada for the full factual background to have come to light, a number of provisional conclusions may be drawn. Firstly, it is clear from the above analysis that serious reservations may be expressed as to the legality of the use of force in this instance. The justifications advanced, both individually and cumulatively, are at best unconvincing.

Secondly, it should be noted that these concerns remain notwithstanding the fact that the present study generally resolved the many serious doctrinal debates, for the purposes of argument, in the manner which was most sympathetic to the legitimacy of the action resorted to by the participating states. A full and objective analysis of the contemporary international law governing the use of force would be unlikely to afford to them such uniformly favourable results.

Finally, it may properly be said, without calling into question the stated motivations of the interested states, that little attention appears to have been paid to considerations of international law in advance of the decision to resort to armed force. The following words of Henkin, spoken some twenty years ago, are seemingly applicable to the situation which this study has sought to address:

"Today everyone still persists in asserting that nations must not intervene in the internal affairs of other nations, and governments continue to accept this principle as law, and may even approve declarations or adhere to conventions incorporating firm prohibitions against intervention. But in regard to the fundamental and dramatic issues of political change, there is no indication that these principles have much relation to the conduct of nations." [186]

---

186 Henkin, supra., note 73, at p. 156.

DOCUMENTATION

APPENDIX NO. 1

DECLARATION OF THE GRENADA REVOLUTION
of 25 March 1979

Source: Declaration of the Grenada Revolution and People's Laws 1979

Whereas constitutional government in Grenada has been interrupted as a consequence of the violations and abuses of democracy committed by the administration of Eric Matthew Gairy under the guise of constitutionality.

And whereas the people of Grenada have expelled the said Gairy from office together with all his Ministers and have appointed in their stead a People's Revolutionary Government for the time being to manage the affairs of Grenada as the Trustees and Executors of the Sovereign powers and rights of the people and have empowered the said People's Revolutionary Government to issue such laws, Orders, Rules and Regulations and to do all things as it may deem necessary for the restoration and preservation of the Peace, Order and good Government of Grenada.

And whereas the People's Revolutionary Government pledges to return to constitutional rule at an early opportunity and to appoint a Consultative Assembly to consult with all the people for the purpose of the establishment of a new Constitution which will reflect the wishes and aspirations of all the people of Grenada. That new Constitution will be submitted for popular approval in a referendum. All sections, classes and strata will be involved.

And whereas during this period of transition the People's Revolutionary Government pledges to observe the fundamental rights and freedoms of our people subject to certain measures necessary to:

(i) The maintenance of stability, peace, order and good government;

(ii) The final eradication of Gairyism; and

(iii) The protection of the People's Revolution.

And whereas on the morning of March 13th 1979 the people of Grenada in the exercise of their sovereignty overthrew the regime of Eric Gairy. This sovereign act of necessity involved the suspension of The Grenada Constitution Order 1973.

And whereas on the 25th day of March, 1979, the following ten People's Laws enacted by the People's Revolutionary Government were orally declared by the Prime Minister and popularly acclaimed.

TREATY ESTABLISHING THE ORGANISATION
OF EASTERN CARIBBEAN STATES (EXTRACTS)
of 18 June, 1981

Source: Secretariat of the Organisation of Eastern Caribbean States, Castries, St. Lucia

Preamble

The Governments of the Contracting States,

convinced that the West Indies (Associated States) Council of Ministers since its establishment in 1966 has done much to further regional co-operation in many fields and has rendered valuable services to its member countries;

recognising that since the establishment of the said Council of Ministers significant constitutional and other changes have taken place in the region;

affirming their determination to achieve economic and social development for their peoples as enunciated in the agreement of the 11th day of June, 1968, establishing the East Caribbean Common Market;

inspired by a common determination to strengthen the links between themselbes by uniting their efforts and resources and establishing and strengthening common institutions which could serve to increase their bargaining power as regards third countries or groupings of countries;

having in mind the strong views expressed by the said Council of Ministers regarding the desirability of retaining and formalising the arrangements for joint action by its member countries;

determined to satisfy the legitimate aspirations of their peoples for development and progress;

have agreed as follows:

Article 1
Establishment of the Organisation of Eastern Caribbean States

By this Treaty the Contracting Parties establish among themselves the Organisation of Eastern Caribbean States (hereinafter called 'The Organisation') having the membership, powers and functions hereinafter specified.

Article 2
Membership

1.

Full membership of the Organisation shall be open to those countries which immediately prior to the establishment of the Organisation have been members of the West Indies (Associated States) Council of Ministers, namely:

(a) Antigua
(b) Dominica
(c) Grenada
(d) Montserrat
(e) St. Kitts/Nevis
(f) Saint Lucia
(g) Saint Vincent and The Grenadines

2.

The independent States listed in the preceding paragraph the Governments of which sign and ratify this Treaty in accordance with Article 20 thereof shall immediately become full members (hereinafter referred to as 'The Member States') of the Organisation.

3.

Notwithstanding that a territory or group of territories listed in Paragraph 1 of this Article is not a sovereign independent State, the Heads of Government of the Member States of the Organisation (hereinafter referred to as 'The Authority') may by a unanimous decision admit such territory or group of territories as a full member of the Organisation and such territory or group of territories shall thereby qualify as a Member State under this Treaty.

4.

Any other States or territories in the Caribbean region may apply to become Full or Associate Members and shall be admitted as such by a unanimous decision of the Authority. The nature and extent of the rights and obligations of Associate Members shall be determined by the Authority.

Article 3
Purposes and Functions of the Organisation

1.

The major purposes of the Organisation shall be:

(a) to promote co-operation among the Member States and at the regional and international levels having due regard to the Treaty establishing the Caribbean Community and the Charter of the United Nations;
(b) to promote unity and solidarity among the Member States and to defend their sovereignty, territorial integrity and independence;
(c) to assist the Member States in the realisation of their obligations and responsibilities to the international community with due regard to the role of international law as a standard of conduct in their relationship;
(d) to seek to achieve the fullest possible harmonisation of foreign policy among the Member States; to seek to adopt, as far as possible, common

positions on international issues and to establish and maintain wherever possible, arrangements for joint overseas representation and/or common services;

(e) to promote economic integration among the Member States through the provisions of the Agreement Establishing the East Caribbean Common Market; and

(f) to pursue the said purposes through its respective institutions by discussion of questions of common concern and by agreement and common action.

2.

To this end the Member States will endeavour to co-ordinate, harmonise and pursue joint policies particularly in the fields of:

(a) External Relations including overseas representation;

(b) International Trade Agreements and other External Economic Relations;

(c) Financial and Technical Assistance from external sources;

(d) International Marketing of Goods and Services including Tourism;

(e) External Transportation and Communications including Civil Aviation;

(f) Economic Integration among the Member States through the provisions of the Agreement Establishing the East Caribbean Common Market;

(g) Matters relating to the sea and its resources;

(h) The Judiciary;

(i) Currency and Central Banking;

(j) Audit;

(k) Statistics;

(l) Income Tax Administration;

(m) Customs and Excise Administration;

(n) Tertiary Education including University;

(o) Training in Public Administration and Management;

(p) Scientific, Technical and Cultural Co-operation;

(q) Mutual Defence and Security; and

(r) Such other activities calculated to further the purposes of the Organisation as the Member States may from time to time decide.

Article 5
Institutions of the Organisation

1.

There are hereby established the following principal institutions through which the Organisation shall accomplish the functions entrusted to it under this Treaty:

(a) The Authority of Heads of Government of the Member States of the Organisation (referred to in this Treaty as 'The Authority');
(b) The Foreign Affairs Committee;
(c) The Defence and Security Committee;
(d) The Economic Affairs Committee; and
(e) The Central Secretariat.

2.

The institutions of the Organisation shall perform the functions and act within the limits of the powers conferred upon them by or under this Treaty and by the Protocols thereto. They may establish such subsidiary institutions as they deem necessary for the performance of their functions.

Article 6

Composition and Functions of the Authority

1. The Authority shall be composed of Heads of Government of the Member States.
2. Any member of the Authority may, as appropriate, designate a Minister to represent such member at any meeting of the Authority.
3. Only Member States possessing the necessary competence in respect of matters under consideration from time to time shall take part in the deliberations of the Authority.
4. The Authority shall be the supreme policy-making institution of the Organisation. It shall be responsible for, and have the general direction and control of the performance of the functions of the Organisation, for the progressive development of the Organisation and the achievement of its purposes.
5. The Authority shall have power to make decisions on all matters within its competence. All such decisions shall require the affirmative vote of all Member States present and voting at the meeting of the Authority at which such decisions were taken provided that such decisions shall have no force and effect until ratified by those Member States, if any, which were not present at that meeting, or until such Member States have notified the Authority of their decision to abstain. Such decisions by the Authority shall be binding on all Member States and on all institutions of the Organisation and effect shall be given to any such decisions provided that it is within the sovereign competence of Member States to implement them.
6. The Authority may make such recommendations and give such directives as it deems necessary for the achievement of the purposes of the Organisation and for ensuring the smooth functioning of the institutions of the Organisation.
7. The Authority may establish, and designate as such, institutions of the Organisation in addition to those specified in sub-paragraphs (b), (c),

(d) and (e) of Paragraph 1 of Article 5 of this Treaty, as it deems necessary for the achievement of the purposes of the Organisation.

8. Subject to the relevant provisions of this Treaty, the Authority shall be the final authority for the conclusion of treaties or other international agreements on behalf of the Organisation and for entering into relationships between the Organisation and other International Organisations and third countries.

9. Subject to the relevant provisions of this Treaty, the Authority shall take decisions for the purpose of establishing the financial arrangements necessary for meeting the expenses of the Organisation and shall be the final authority on questions arising in relation to the financial affairs of the Organisation.

10. The Authority shall meet at least twice a year. It shall determine its own procedure including that for convening meetings, for the conduct of business thereat and at other times, and for the annual rotation of the office of Chairman among its members in accordance with the principle of alphabetical order of the Member States.

11. The Authority shall in addition meet in extraordinary session whenever it deems necessary in accordance with the regulations laid down in its rules of procedure.

Article 7
Composition and Functions of the Foreign Affairs Committee

1. The Foreign Affairs Committee shall consist of the Ministers responsible for Foreign Affairs in the Governments of the Member States or such other Ministers as may be designated by the Heads of Government of the Member States.

2. Only Member States possessing the necessary competence in respect of matters under consideration from time to time shall take part in the deliberations of the Foreign Affairs Committee.

3. The Foreign Affairs Committee shall be responsible to the Authority. It shall take appropriate action on any matters referred to it by the Authority and shall have the power to make recommendations to the Authority.

4. The Foreign Affairs Committee shall have responsibility for the progressive development of the foreign policy of the Organisation and for the general direction and control of the performance of the executive functions of the Organisation in relation to its foreign affairs.

5. The decisions and directives of the Foreign Affairs Committee shall be unanimous and shall be binding on all subordinate institutions of the Organisation unless otherwise determined by the Authority.

6. Subject to any directives that the Authority may give, the Foreign Affairs Committee shall meet as and when necessary. It shall determine

its own procedure, including that for convening meetings, for the conduct of business thereat, and at other times and for the annual rotation of the office of Chairman among its members in accordance with the principle of alphabetical order of the Member States.

Article 8
Composition and Functions of the Defence and Security Committee

1. The Defence and Security Committee shall consist of the Ministers responsible for Defence and Security or other Ministers or Plenipotentiaries designated by Heads of Government of the Member States.

2. Only Member States possessing the necessary competence in respect of matters under consideration from time to time shall take part in the deliberations of the Defence and Security Committee.

3. The Defence and Security Committee shall be responsible to the Authority. It shall take appropriate action on any matters referred to it by the Authority and shall have the power to make recommendations to the Authority. It shall advise the Authority on matters relating to external defence and on arrangements for collective security against external aggression, including mercenary aggression, with or without the support of internal or national elements.

4. The Defence and Security Committee shall have responsibility for coordinating the efforts of Member States for collective defence and the preservation of peace and security against external aggression and for the development of close ties among the Member States of the Organisation in matters of external defence and security, including measures to combat the activities of mercenaries, operating with or without the support of internal or national elements, in the exercise of the inherent right of individual or collective self-defence recognised by Article 51 of the Charter of the United Nations.

5. The decisions and directives of the Defence and Security Committee shall be unanimous and shall be binding on all subordinate institutions of the Organisation unless otherwise determined by the Authority.

6. Subject to any directives that the Authority may give, the Defence and Security Committee shall meet as and when necessary. It shall determine its own procedure, including that for convening meetings, for the conduct of business thereat and at other times, and for the annual rotation of the Office of Chairman among its members in accordance with the principle of alphabetical order of the Member States.

Article 11
Co-ordination and Harmonisation of Foreign Policy

1. Unless objection is offered by the receiving States or international organisations and conferences concerned, Member States of the Organisation may establish and maintain arrangements for joint overseas diplomatic or other representation, including, where appropriate, the accreditation of one representative to one or more States, international organisations or conferences.

2. Where such objection, referred to in the preceding paragraph, is made by an international organisation or conference by virtue of its constitution or rules of procedure or for any other reason and where the Member States are members of such organisation or conference, the Director-General shall take all appropriate steps, consistent with the constitution or fules of procedure of such organisation or conference, as to ensure the optimum realisation of the benefits of their membership of such organisation or conference.

3. The Director-General shall have the authority and responsibility for transmitting directives of the Authority on joint foreign policy matters to heads of overseas diplomatic and other missions established by the Organisation. He shall take precedence in matters of protocol over the heads of such missions.

4. Heads of diplomatic or other missions of the Organisation shall be recommended for appointment by the Authority after consultation with the Foreign Affairs Committee. Provided that they may at any time resign their offices by written notice to the Director-General, who shall promptly transmit such notice to the Member States of the Organisation.

5. Subject to the preceding paragraph, the staff of such missions shall be appointed by the Director-General. In appointing such staff he shall have due regard to the provisions of Paragraphs 6 and 7 of Article 10 of this Treaty. The terms and conditions of service of such staff shall be governed by such rules and regulations as govern the staff at the headquarters of the Organisation.

6. The expenses for diplomatic or other representatives referred to in Paragraph 1 of this Article shall be apportioned among the Member States participating in such arrangements.

Article 14
Procedure for the Settlement of Disputes

1. Any dispute that may arise between two or more of the Member States regarding the interpretation and application of this Treaty shall, upon the request of any of them, be amicably resolved by direct agreement.
2. If the dispute is not resolved within three months of the date on which the request referred to in the preceding paragraph has been made, any party to the dispute may submit it to the conciliation procedure provided for in Annex A to this Treaty by submitting a request to that effect to the Director-General of the Organisation and informing the other party or parties to the dispute of the request.
3. Member States undertake to accept the conciliation procedure referred to in the preceding paragraph as compulsory. Any decisions or recommendations of the Conciliation Commission in resolution of the dispute shall be final and binding on the Member States.

Article 15
Participation in other Arrangements

1. Nothing in this Treaty shall preclude any Member State from participating in other arrangements either with other Member States or non-Member States provided that its participation in such arrangements does not derogate from the provisions of this Treaty.
2. The rights and obligations arising from agreements concluded before the entry into force of this Treaty between Member States, or between Member States and other countries or organisations shall not be affected by the provisions of this Treaty.
3. To the extent that such agreements are not compatible with this Treaty, the Member State or States concerned shall take all appropriate steps to eliminate the incompatibilities established. Member States shall, where necessary, assist each other to this end and shall, where appropriate, adopt a common attitude.

Article 22
Admission to Membership. Accession and Adherence

1. After this Treaty has entered into force in accordance with the provisions of Article 21 thereof, any independent State or Territory specified in Article 2 of this Treaty may apply to the Authority to become a Full Member or Associate Member of the Organisation and may, if the Authority so decides, be admitted as such in accordance with Paragraphs 3 and 4 of Article 2 of this Treaty respectively.

83

2. Unless otherwise desired by the Authority, admission to full membership of the Organisation shall take effect immediately upon a decision to that effect by the Authority.
3. Each Territory admitted to full membership of the Organisation shall accede to this Treaty in accordance with the provisions of Paragraph 4 of Article 20 thereof upon its attainment of independent statehood.
4. Any independent State or Territory in the Caribbean region may at any time notify the Director-General of its intention to adhere to this Treaty.
5. The Director-General shall, on receipt of such notification, transmit a copy of it to all the signatories and to the Government of Saint Lucia.
6. The terms and conditions of adherence in any particular case shall be determined by the Authority.

Article 23
Declaration of Non-Participation

Any Member State may, either on becoming a member of the Organisation or within a period not exceeding twelve (12) months thereafter, declare in writing to the Director-General its intention to withhold its participation in respect of Foreign Affairs and/or Defence and Security matters of the Organisation. The Director-General shall on receipt of such declaration promptly transmit a copy of it to all the other Member States of the Organisation. Such declaration shall take effect on the date of its receipt by the Director-General.

Article 24
Withdrawal

1. This Treaty shall be of unlimited duration.
2. Any Member State, whether a Full Member or an Associate Member, may withdraw from the Organisation if it decides that extraordinary events, related to the subject-matter of this Treaty, have seriously endangered its supreme national interests. It shall give written notice of such withdrawal to the Director-General who shall promptly notify the other Member States and the Government of Saint Lucia. Such withdrawal shall take effect twelve (12) months after the notice is received by the Director-General.
3. Any Member State which withdraws from the Organisation shall discharge its financial obligations to the Organisation and shall respect any commitments undertaken before the effective date of withdrawal.

Article 26
Registration

This Treaty and all its Protocols shall be registered by the Government of Saint Lucia with the Secretariat of the United Nations pursuant to Article 102 of the Charter of the United Nations and shall also be registered with the Secretariat of the Caribbean Community.

In witness whereof, the Undersigned Plenipotentiaries, being duly authorised thereto by their respective Governments, have signed the present Treaty.

Done at Basseterre this Eighteenth day of June, One thousand nine hundred and eighty-one.

For the Government of:

Antigua	*Lester Bird*
Dominica	*M. Eugenia Charles*
Grenada	*Maurice Bishop*
Montserrat	*F.A.L. Margetson*
St. Kitts/Nevis	*Kennedy A. Simmonds*
Saint Lucia	*Winston F. Cenac*
Saint Vincent and The Grenadines	*Hudson Tannis*

ANNEX A
Conciliation Commission

1.

A list of conciliators consisting of qualified jurists shall be drawn up and maintained by the Director-General of the Organisation. To this end, every Member State shall be invited to nominate two conciliators, and the names of the persons so nominated shall constitute the list. The term of a conciliator, including that of any conciliator nominated to fill a casual vacancy, shall be five years and may be renewed. A conciliator whose term expires shall continue to fulfil any function for which he shall have been chosen under the following paragraph.

2.

(a) When a request has been made to the Director-General under Article 14, the Director-General shall bring the dispute before a Conciliation Commission constituted as follows:

The Member State or Member States constituting one of the parties to the dispute shall appoint:

  (i) one conciliator who is a citizen of that State or of one of those

States and who may or may not be chosen from the list referred to in paragraph 1; and

(ii) one conciliator who is not a citizen of that State or of any of those States and who shall be chosen from the list.

(b) The Member State or Member States constituting the other party to the dispute shall appoint two conciliators in the same way. The four conciliators chosen by the parties shall be appointed within thirty days following the date on which the Director-General received the request.

(c) The four conciliators shall, within thirty days following the date of the last of their own appointments, appoint a fifth conciliator chosen from the list, who shall be chairman.

(d) If the appointment of the Chairman or of any of the other conciliators has not been made within the period prescribed above for such appointment, it shall be made by the Director-General within thirty days following the expiry of that period. The appointment of the Chairman may be made by the Director-General either from the list or from the membership of the International Law Commission. Any of the periods within which appointments must be made may be extended by agreement between the parties to the dispute.

(e) Any vacancy shall be filled in the manner prescribed for the initial appointment.

3.

The Conciliation Commission shall decide its own procedure. The Commission, with the consent of the parties to the dispute, may invite any Member State of the Organisation to submit to it its views orally or in writing. Decisions and recommendations of the Commission shall be made by a majority vote of the five members.

4.

The Commission may draw the attention of the parties to the dispute to any measures which might facilitate an amicable settlement.

5.

The Commission shall hear the parties, examine the claims and objections, and make proposals to the parties with a view to reaching an amicable settlement of the dispute.

6.

The Commission shall report within six months of its constitution. Its report shall be deposited with the Director-General and transmitted to the parties to the dispute. The report of the Commission, including any conclusions stated therein regarding the facts or questions of law, shall be binding upon the parties.

7.

The Director-General shall provide the Commission with such assistance and facilitates as it may require. The expenses of the Commission shall be borne by the Organisation.

APPENDIX NO. 3

DECLARATION OF NON-PARTICIPATION
BY THE COLONY OF MONTSERRAT UNDER ARTICLE 23
OF THE TREATY ESTABLISHING THE ORGANISATION
OF EASTERN CARIBBEAN STATES
Undated

Source: Foreign and Commonwealth Office, London, U.K.

Whereas the Treaty Establishing the Organisation of Eastern Caribbean States was signed on behalf of the Government of Montserrat by the Honourable F.A.L. Margetson, Minister of Agriculture, Trade, Lands and Housing on the 18th day of June 1981,

and whereas at a meeting of the Authority of Heads of Government of the Member States of the Organisation held in St. Lucia on December 12th 1981 Montserrat was admitted as a Member State of the Organisation in accordance with Article 2.2 of the Treaty,

and whereas Article 23 of the Treaty provides that any Member State may, on becoming a member of the Organisation, declare in writing to the Director-General its intention to withhold its participation in respect of Foreign Affairs and/or Defence and Security matters of the Organisation,

now therefore this Declaration is to notify the Director-General of the Organisation that it is the intention of the Colony of Montserrat to withhold its participation in respect of Foreign Affairs and Defence and Security matters of the Organisation, to the extent that any decisions of the Organisation or any committee or institution thereof may require action to be taken by the Government of Montserrat inconsistent with the views, directives, policies and obligations of Her Majesty's Government of the United Kingdom.

'MEMORANDUM OF UNDERSTANDING'
(BETWEEN ANTIGUA AND BARBUDA, BARBADOS, DOMINICA, ST. LUCIA AND ST. VINCENT AND THE GRENADINES)
'RELATING TO SECURITY AND MILITARY CO-OPERATION'
(EXTRACTS)
of 29 October, 1982

Areas of Co-operation

2. The parties hereto agree to prepare contingency plans and assist one another on request in national emergencies, prevention of smuggling, search and rescue, immigration control, maritime policing duties, protection of off-shore installations, pollution control, natural and other disasters and threats to national security.

3. With regard to paragraph 2, the interests of one participating country are the interests of the others; and accordingly the participating countries shall have the right of "hot-pursuit" within each other's territorial waters.

Council of Ministers

4. The Ministers responsible for Defence in the participating countries shall be the Council of Ministers, which shall be the central policy making body.

5. The Council of Ministers may appoint advisory Committees comprising such persons from the participating countries as might be necessary.

6. The Council of Ministers shall meet at least once a year.

Central Liaison Office

7. There shall be a Central Liaison Office, which shall be responsible to the Council of Ministers for co-ordinating the objectives of this Memorandum of Understanding.

8. There shall be a Regional Security Co-ordinator, who shall be the chief officer of the Central Liaison Office; and there shall be such other staff as the Council of Ministers shall determine.

9. The Regional Security Co-ordinator shall be appointed by the Council of Ministers.

10. Staff, other than the Regional Security Co-ordinator, shall be appointed by the Council of Ministers on the recommendation of the Regional Security Co-ordinator after consultation with the Forces Commanders.

11. The Regional Security Co-ordinator shall also be adviser to the Council of Ministers in matters relating to regional security and shall be authorised

to negotiate with extra-regional agencies on behalf of the parties hereto; but any negotiation conducted by the Regional Security Co-ordinator does not bind the Government of any participating country unless ratified in writing by the Government of that participating country.

12. The salaries of the staff of the Central Liaison Office shall be fixed from time to time by the Council of Ministers.

Planning and Operations

17. There shall be a joint co-ordinating and planning committee comprising the Forces Commanders.

18. Combined operations shall be co-ordinated through the operations room at the Barbados Defence Force Headquarters, St. Ann's Fort, Barbados or such other suitable place as may be agreed between the Forces Commanders.

19. The manning of the operations room shall be agreed between the Forces Commanders.

Command and Discipline

20. For the purposes of this Memorandum of Understanding,
    (a) the requesting country shall retain operational control over all troops participating in operations in that country;
    (b) the senior officer of the sending country shall exercise tactical command over his troops;
    (c) commanding officers shall be responsible for the conduct and discipline of their subordinate service personnel.

Jurisdiction

21. When service personnel of one participating country are within the jurisdiction of another participating country, they shall respect the laws, customs and traditions of that other participating country.

22. (1) The Service Authorities of one participating country shall have, within another participating country or on board any vessel or aircraft of that other country, the right to exercise all such criminal and disciplinary jurisdiction over its service personnel, as are conferred on the Service Authorities by the laws of their own country, including the right to repatriate personnel to their own country for trial and sentencing.

(2) The Courts of one participating country shall have jurisdiction over service personnel of another participating country with respect to offences that are committed by the service personnel of that other participating country within the first-mentioned participating country and punishable by the law of the first-mentioned participating country.

(3) Where the Courts of one participating country and the Service Authorities of another participating country have the right to exercise jurisdiction in respect of an offence, the Service Authorities of that other participating country shall have the primary right to exercise jurisdiction if

    (i) the offence is committed by a member of the service personnel of that other participating country against the property or security of that other participating country or against the property or person of another member of the service personnel, or

    (ii) the offence arises out of an act or omission arising in the course of official duty by a member of the service personnel of that other participating country.

(4) In any case other than those mentioned in sub-paragraphs (1), (2) and (3) the participating country within which the offence is committed shall have the primary right to exercise jurisdiction; but where the country with the primary right decides not to exercise jurisdiction, it shall notify the appropriate authorities of the other country as soon as practicable.

Claims

23. The government of each of the participating countries shall insure its service personnel against any claims for damage or injury, including injury resulting in death, caused by acts or omissions of its service personnel in the course of their duties.

24. In the case of an omission by a participating country to insure its service personnel, or where for any other reason service personnel of a participating country are not covered by insurance, that participating country shall deal with and settle at its own cost any claim brought by any person in respect of damage or injury arising out of the course of official duty.

25. If the law of one participating country does not preserve, save and keep free a member of the service personnel of another participating country against damages for a claim to which paragraph 23 or 24 relates, the first-mentioned participating country undertakes to preserve, save and keep him free from any such damages.

26. The participating country within whose jurisdiction any damage or injury occurs shall settle any claim brought in respect thereof, and where the damage was done or the injury caused by the personnel of any other participating country that other country shall re-imburse the first-mentioned country.

Training

27. Service personnel of the participating countries shall undergo training in any of the participating countries on agreement between the Forces

Commanders of the participating countries involved in the training exercise.

28. In training operations the Coast Guard units shall be permitted to enter each other's territorial waters on agreement between the Forces Commanders of the countries participating in the training operations.

29. Where necessary, exchange billets shall be by mutual agreement between the Forces Commanders of the units participating in the exchange.

Procurement

36. By agreement between the Forces Commanders arms, ammunition, uniforms, equipment and stores may be procured under a joint procurement programme.

37. Arms, ammunition, uniforms, equipment and stores procured under the joint procurement programme mentioned in paragraph 36 shall be transferred among the participating countries by agreement between the Forces Commanders.

Operational Expenses

38. For the purposes of this Memorandum of Understanding
   (a) the requesting country shall pay
      (i) the expenses incurred in accommodating and victualling the troops of the sending country, and
      (ii) the medical expenses of any troops of the sending country who need medical attention in the requesting country;
   (b) each participating country shall meet its own fuel costs;
   (c) each participating country shall meet the cost of materials used in training its service personnel; and
   (d) each participating country shall meet the costs of materials and labour used in maintaining its vessels.

Limited Assistance

39. A participating country may request assistance from one or more of the other participating countries and where such a request is made
   (a) the Ministers responsible for Defence in those participating countries, and
   (b) the Forces Commanders of those participating countries,
constitute, respectively, the Council of Ministers and the Forces Commanders for that limited purpose only; and this Memorandum of Understanding shall be read and construed accordingly.

Territorial Waters, Exclusive Economic Zone and Visiting Forces

40. The Governments of the participating countries shall review and update their laws
  (a) relating to their territorial waters and their exclusive economic zones, and
  (b) relating to armed forces visiting the participating countries.

APPENDIX NO. 5

ORGANISATION OF EASTERN CARIBBEAN STATES:
PRESS RELEASE
Undated but related to the Heads of Government Meeting
of 21 October, 1983

Source: Secretariat of the Organisation of Eastern Caribbean States,
Castries, St. Lucia

Heads of Government of the Organisation of Eastern Caribbean States, meeting as the Authority of the Organisation in Barbados on 21st October 1983, decided on the following measures to be taken as sanctions against the Military Regime in Grenada: —

  (I) No official contact with the existing Regime:
  "Measures for ensuring the safety of nationals of other OECS states to be undertaken by international agencies such as the Red Cross at the request of governments concerned"

 (II) The Regime would not be permitted to participate in the deliberations and business of the Organisation:

(III) Representatives of the Regime would not be permitted to participate in or chair caucuses or groupings pertaining to meetings of international agencies, and would not be permitted to speak on behalf of the OECS in international agencies:

(IV) The Regime would not be allowed to benefit from the trade, economic and functional co-operation arrangements of the Organisation:

 (V) No new issues of currency will be made to the Regime under the Eastern Caribbean Central Bank (ECCB) Arrangement:

(VI) The OECS Governments will cease all sea and air communication links with Grenada until further notice.

DIPLOMATIC NOTE FROM THE GRENADA REVOLUTIONARY COUNCIL TO THE EMBASSY OF THE UNITED STATES IN BARBADOS (TEXT AS BROADCAST BY RADIO FREE GRENADA)
of 23 October, 1983

Source: 'Barbados Advocate' (Bridgetown, Barbados, 25 October, 1983

The Ministry of Foreign Affairs of the Revolutionary Military Council of Grenada presents its compliments to the honourable Embassy of the United States in Barbados and takes this opportunity to express concern to the honourable embassy.

It is our information that at a meeting of some CARICOM Governments in Port-of-Spain, Trinidad, on Sunday, October 23, 1983, some of the participating governments decided on establishing a military force to invade Grenada. In their decision, they called for direct participation of extra-regional forces in invading Grenada.

We are concerned because in many reports, the name of the Government of the United States of America has been mentioned as participating in such a military force to invade our country. We have had concrete information that for the past 10 hours two warships have been patrolling between 12 to 15 kilometres off the shores of Grenada well within our territorial waters.

We would view any invasion of our country whether based on the decisions of those CARICOM Governments or by that of any other government as a rude violation of Grenada's sovereignty and of international law.

Furthermore, any such invasion can only lead to the loss of lives of thousands of men, women and children. Therefore we strongly condemn such a decision. The present situation in Grenada is of an entirely internal and domestic nature and presently peace, calm and good order prevail in our country.

For these reasons we do not understand the basis or the reasons for the reported violent reaction of some Caribbean and other governments. We view any threat or the use of force by any country or group of countries as a gross and unwarranted interference in the domestic affairs of our sovereign and independent country.

Grenada has not and is not threatening the use of force against any country and we do not have such aspirations. Our armed forces and people are fully prepared to courageously defend the sovereignty and integrity of our country with dignity and determination.

However we are not seeking military confrontation with other countries or group of countries but on the contrary we are prepared to hold discussions with those countries in order to ensure good relations and mutual understanding and with a view towards maintaining and strengthening the historic ties with all of these countries.

We are also concerned about reports that the Government of the United States of America is considering sending battleships to evacuate citizens of their countries presently residing peacefully in Grenada. We reiterate that the lives, well-being and property of every American and other foreign citizens residing in Grenada are fully protected and guaranteed by our government.

However, any American or foreign citizen in our country who desires to leave Grenada for whatever reasons can fully do so using the normal procedures through our airports on commercial aircraft. As far as we are concerned, these aircraft can be regular flights or chartered flights and we will facilitate them in every way we can.

We have been further informed that 500 parents of American students studying in Grenada at the St. Georges University School of Medicine yesterday met in New York and unanimously agreed on a resolution calling on the United States of America Administration not to take precipitous and provocative action against Grenada.

We have also been informed during the last two hours by Dr. Geoffrey Bourne, vice-chancellor of the St. Georges University School of Medicine where most of the U.S. citizens are based that less than 10 per cent of these students wish to leave Grenada at this time.

In fact, Dr. Bourne stated this in his own voice with Radio Free Grenada in a telephone conversation with the newsroom less than three hours ago. We further assure you that any U.S. and other foreign citizens who choose to leave Grenada in the coming days and who wish to return to Grenada in the future are welcome to do so.

We are for peace, friendship and for maintaining historically established ties between our countries and hope they would grow and further strengthen. We further take this opportunity to inform your government that the Revolutionary Military Council of Grenada has no desire or aspiration to rule the country.

We have already held discussions with our local Chamber of Commerce and Industry, commercial bank managers and hoteliers, as part of the process of constituting such a government.

Our civilian government will pursue mixed economy with state co-operatives and private sectors and would encourage foreign and local investment within the framework of the national interest of the country. In closing we wish to state once more that there is absolutely no basis whatsoever for any countries launching an invasion of our beloved country.

The Ministry of Foreign Affairs of the Revolutionary Military Council of Grenada takes this opportunity to reassure the honourable Embassy of the United States of America the testimony of its most distinguished and highest regard.

LETTER FROM THE GOVERNOR-GENERAL OF GRENADA
TO THE PRIME MINISTER OF BARBADOS
Date: Uncertain

Source: 'The Times' (London, U.K.), 10 November, 1983

Dear Prime Minister,

You are aware that there is a vacuum of authority in Grenada following the killing of the Prime Minister and the subsequent serious violations of human rights and bloodshed.

I am therefore seriously concerned over the lack of internal security in Grenada. Consequently I am requesting your help to assist me in stabilizing this grave and dangerous situation. It is my desire that a peace-keeping force should be established in Grenada to facilitate a rapid return to peace and tranquility and also a return to democratic rule.

In this connexion I am also seeking assistance from the United States, from Jamaica, and from the Organization of Eastern Caribbean States through its current chairman the hon. Eugenia Charles (Prime Minister of Dominica) in the spirit of the treaty establishing that organization to which my country is a signatory.

I have the honour to be,
Yours faithfully,
Paul Scoon,
Governor-General.

APPENDIX NO. 8

DRAFT SECURITY COUNCIL RESOLUTION
(GUYANA AND NICARAGUA) ON THE SITUATION IN GRENADA
of 25 October, 1983

Source: United Nations Information Centre, London, U.K.

The Security Council,

Having heard the statements made in connection with the situation in Grenada,

Recalling the Declaration on Principles of International Law concerning friendly relations and co-operation among States,

Recalling also the Declaration on the Inadmissibility of Intervention and Interference in the internal affairs of States,

Reaffirming the sovereign and inalienable right of Grenada freely to determine its own political, economic, and social system and to develop its international relations without outside intervention, interference, subversion, coercion or threat in any form whatsoever,

Deeply deploring the events in Grenada which led to the killing of the Prime Minister, Mr. Maurice Bishop, and other prominent Grenadians,

Bearing in mind that, in accordance with Article 2 (4) of the United Nations Charter, all Member States are obliged to refrain in their international relations from the threat or use of force against the sovereignty, territorial integrity or political independence of any State or to act in any other manner inconsistent with the principles and purposes of the Charter of the United Nations,

Gravely concerned at the military intervention taking place and determined to ensure a speedy return to normalcy in Grenada,

Conscious of the need for States to show consistent respect for the principles of the United Nations Charter,

1. *Strongly condemns* the armed intervention in Grenada which constitutes a flagrant violation of international law and of the independence, sovereignty and territorial integrity of that State;

2. *Deplores* the deaths of innocent civilians resulting from the shelling and bombardment of Grenada including built-up civilian population areas, and from other acts by the invading force;

3. *Calls on* all States to show strictest respect for the sovereignty, independence and territorial integrity of Grenada;

4. *Calls for* an immediate cessation of intervention and the immediate withdrawal of the invading troops from Grenada;

5. *Requests* the Secretary-General to follow closely the development of the situation in Grenada and to report to the Council within 48 hours on the implementation of this resolution.

ORGANISATION OF EASTERN CARIBBEAN STATES: STATEMENT ON THE GRENADA SITUATION
of 25 October, 1983

Source: Secretariat of the Organisation of Eastern Caribbean States,
Castries, St. Lucia

The Member Governments of the Organisation of Eastern Caribbean States met at Bridgetown, Barbados on Friday, 21st October 1983 to consider and evaluate the situation in Grenada arising out of the overthrow of Prime Minister Maurice Bishop and the subsequent killing of the Prime Minister together with some of his Cabinet colleagues and a number of other citizens.

The Member States were deeply concerned that this situation would continue to worsen; that there would be further loss of life, personal injury and a general deterioration of public order as the military group in control attempted to secure its position.

Member Governments considered that the subsequent imposition of a draconial 96 hour curfew by the military group in control was intended to allow them to further suppress the population of Grenada which had shown by numerous demonstrations their hostility to this group.

Member Governments are also greatly concerned that the extensive military build up in Grenada over the last few years had created a situation of disproportionate military strength between Grenada and other OECS countries. This military might in the hands of the present group posed a serious threat to the security of the OECS countries and other neighbouring States. Member Governments considered it of the utmost urgency that immediate steps should be taken to remove this threat.

Under the provisions of Article 8 of the Treaty establishing the OECS, concerning Defence and Security in the sub-region, Member Governments of the Organisation therefore decided to take appropriate action.

Bearing in mind the relative lack of military resources in the possession of the other OECS countries, the Member Governments have sought assistance for this purpose from friendly countries within the region and subsequently from outside.

Three governments have responded to the OECS Member Governments' request to form a multi-national force for the purpose of undertaking a pre-emptive defensive strike in order to remove this dangerous threat to the peace and security of their sub-region and to establish a situation of normality in Grenada. These governments are Barbados, Jamaica and the United States of America. Barbados and Jamaica are members of Caricom and Barbados is linked to some of the OECS Member Governments in a Sub-regional Securing Agreement.

It is the intention of the Member Governments of the OECS, that once the threat has been removed they will invite the Governor-General of Grenada to assume executive authority of the country under the provisions of the Grenada Constitution of 1973 and to appoint a broad-based *interim government* to administer the country pending the holding of General Elections.

It has been agreed that while these arrangements are being put in place, the presence of former Prime Minister Eric Gairy and others who might further complicate the situation, would therefore not be welcomed in Grenada.

It is further intended that arrangements should be made to establish effective police and peace keeping forces in order to restore and maintain law and order in the country.

After normalcy has been restored, non-Caribbean forces will be invited to withdraw from Grenada.

Member Governments of the Organisation of Eastern Caribbean States wish to solicit the diplomatic support of all friendly countries for this initiative.

APPENDIX NO. 10

ADDRESS TO THE JAMAICAN HOUSE OF REPRESENTATIVES BY PRIME MINISTER SEAGA (EXTRACTS)
of 25 October, 1983

Source: 'The Daily Gleaner' (Kingston, Jamaica), 26 October, 1983

The purpose of the military operation now under way in Grenada is to restore the country to normality with a minimum loss of lives, to free the people of Grenada from terrorism and brutality which they have been suffering and to eliminate the perceived threat of hostility and aggression by Grenada to neighbouring Caribbean states caused by nations unfriendly to the cause of democracy which were at the seat of influence in the affairs of the island.

During the past week, we witnessed in Grenada not only a revolution spawning its own destruction but a brutal military take-over of a civilian Government.

It may be felt that these matters do not concern us; but most certainly they do. If a whole Government can be wiped out overnight either by political or military extremists and the Governments of the Caribbean remain silent and passive, then no Government elected by the people can be safe from madmen of one type or another who would seek to replace a Government of the people, elected by the people with one selected by a chosen few of whatever nature.

If we ignore the occurrence of brutal military take-overs or political overthrows of Governments, we would immediately give heart to every subversive group within the region to engineer disorders and instability as a means of overthrows. No democratic system of Government would have a chance of carrying out the programmes of development which it was elected to implement if in its midst was a group of subversives, anarchists and terrorists bent on destruction of the foundations of stability which under-pin the whole system of democracy. The far-reaching consequences of such neglect on our part would be awesome, and would have the effect of creating an unsure and insecure future for all of us.

For the sake of the democratic system of Government which we all agree to be the one which allows the maximum freedom of choice to a people and protects their right to elect a Government of their choice, we cannot ignore the events which defeat these purposes wherever they occur in the English-speaking Caribbean.

In the states in the Eastern Caribbean there is at this moment not only a strong revulsion against the recent atrocities in Grenada, which we share, but also overwhelming anxiety — indeed fear — for their own security. This added urgency to the need to find a solution to the Grenada crisis.

The time has now come when the English-speaking Caribbean countries have made it unmistakably clear that we will not tolerate subversion and revolution, and that we will take the necessary action to deal with all such instances emphatically and decisively.

There is no question that events since the 13th of October mark a turning point in the history of the English-speaking Caribbean, and it is equally certain that the aftermath of these events will leave none of us untouched.

We have had to take action to defend our deepest values for the maintenance of our own self-respect in helping our sister nations in the Eastern Caribbean to preserve their peace and security.

The events in Grenada fall into two parts: the total breakdown of internal order as a result of the killing of the Prime Minister and almost the entire Cabinet, leaving a vacuum of authority which was filled by men of the most brutal type who proceeded to commit atrocities against people and even little children, leading to a large, and as yet undetermined number of deaths.

The external component of this tragedy is based on the perceived threat arising from the capacity of the leadership which seized power, to use the armed capabilities and military infrastructure of Grenada for acts of hostility against neighbouring states.

Who then can blame the Eastern Caribbean states for perceiving this combination of awesome might and brutal men, who apparently had no concept of where to stop in taking human life, as a prelude to hostile action being taken, beyond their own borders by those in power in Grenada?

These considerations are set out in a document presented by the Authority of the Organisation of Eastern Caribbean States, with an accompanying letter as the basis of the invitation to friendly Governments to come to their aid in restoring normality to Grenada and in removing the perceived threat to peace and security in their region.

I set out here the contents of the annexure to the letter of invitation:

1. The Authority of the Organisation of Eastern Caribbean States (O.E.C.S.) met at Bridgetown, Barbados, on Friday, 21st October, 1983, to consider and evaluate the situation in Grenada arising out of the overthrow of the Government led by Prime Minister together with some of his colleagues and a number of other citizens.

2. The Authority is aware that the overthrow of the Bishop administration took place with the knowledge and connivance of forces unfriendly to the O.E.C.S., leading to the establishment of the present military regime.

3. The meeting took note of the current anarchical conditions, the serious violations of human rights and bloodshed that have occurred, and the consequent unprecedented threat to the peace and security of the region created by the vacuum of authority in Grenada.

4. The Authority was deeply concerned that military forces and supplies are likely to be shortly introduced to consolidate the position of the regime and that the country can be used as a staging post for acts of aggression against its members.

5. The Authority further noted that the capability of the Grenada armed forces is already at a level of sophistication and size far beyond the internal needs of that country. Furthermore the member states of the OECS have no means of defence against such forces.

6. The member governments of the Organisation hold the strong view that such a situation would further undermine political, social and economic stability, and would have extremely dangerous consequences for the preservation of peace and security in the OECS sub-region as a whole.

7. The Authority noted that the present regime in Grenada has demon-

strated by its brutality and ruthlessness that it will stop at nothing to achieve its ends and to secure its power.

8. Under the Authority of Article 8 of the treaty establishing the Organisation of Eastern Caribbean States, the Authority proposes therefore to take action for collective defence and the preservation of peace and security against external aggression by requesting assistance from friendly countries to provide transport, logistics support and additional military personnel to assist the efforts of the O.E.C.S. to stabilise this most grave situation within the eastern Caribbean.

9. The Authority of the O.E.C.S. wishes to establish a peacekeeping force with the assistance of friendly neighbouring states to restore on Grenada conditions of tranquility and order so as to prevent further loss of life and abuses of human rights pending the restoration of constitutional government.

The letter itself reads as follows:

Dear Prime Minister,

The Chairman of the Organisation of Eastern Caribbean States presents her compliments to the Rt. Honourable Edward Seaga, Prime Minister of Jamaica, and has the honour to transmit herewith a request for assistance under Article 8 of the treaty establishing the Organisation of Eastern Caribbean States.

The Chairman of the Organisation of Eastern Caribbean States avails herself of this opportunity to renew the assurances of her highest consideration.

Sincerely
(Sgd.) Eugenia Charles
Chairman
Organisation of Eastern Caribbean States
23rd October, 1983.

It was on this basis that the Government of Jamaica decided to engage its defence force in a multinational military action to carry out a preemptive strike to remove the threat to peace and security in the area and at the same time to restore normality to the island of Grenada.

ADDRESS TO THE BARBARDIAN PEOPLE
BY PRIME MINISTER ADAMS (EXTRACTS)
of 26 October, 1983

Source: 'Barbados Advocate' (Bridgetown, Barbados), 28 October, 1983

This evening I want to analyse and describe for the benefit of our nation, our neighbours and those outside the Caribbean, the circumstances that have led to the joint action taken in the last few days to restore law, order and constitutional government in Grenada and a measure of peace and security in our part of the Caribbean.

On Friday, October 14, our Foreign Ministry was informed by a friendly diplomatic source — not the United States — that, following ideological disagreement, Maurice Bishop had been placed under house arrest and that Bernard Coard would be taking over as Prime Minister. This was apparently announced in St. Georges, but was very badly received by the Grenadian People. I considered that house arrest of a Prime Minister was an act so extreme as to imply some measure of imminent violence and disorder, and when that afternoon I was notified that Unison Whiteman, Grenada's Foreign Minister, was in Barbados intransit to Grenada I made arrangements to speak to him on the telephone. I suggested to him that it might not be safe to return home and that he would be welcome to stay in Barbados, indeed to have political asylum if he wished. We spoke cordially, but he declined my offer and returned home, that afternoon.

A further day of confusion in Grenada followed while some of us discussed the situation. I concluded that, whatever our differences in the past, Mr. Bishop deserved the support of Caribbean governments in the circumstances and sought opinion on whether he could be got out of the hands of his enemies and the situation given an opportunity to stabilise. On this day also, Saturday, October 15, an official of the Ministry of Defence and Security reported to me that he had been tentatively approached by a United States official about the prospect of rescuing Maurice Bishop from his captors and had been made an offer of transport.

An emergency meeting of the Barbados cabinet was held on Wednesday, October 19, to consider what steps should be taken to deal with the obviously deteriorating situation. It was agreed to proceed with a rescue plan, in collaboration with Eastern Caribbean countries and larger non-Caribbean countries with the resources necessary to carry out such an intricate operation.

As we all now know, this proved to be in vain. While we were sitting in

Cabinet the crowd rescued Bishop and led him unwittingly to his brutal death at the hands of his political opponents. Many of his Cabinet died with him. So did innocent men, women and children. Grenada descended into a brutal anarchy, with no government and no institutions other than those maintained by the whim of a gang of murderers.

The very next day, Thursday 20 October, I was telephoned by Prime Minister Compton of St. Lucia, who expressed himself in the strongest possible terms that the situation in Grenada could not remain as it was, and he proposed that there be a Caribbean initiative to intervene in Grenada on a multi-national basis to restore law and order and to lead the country to an early election. He emphasised that the entire Caribbean be invited to join and then to seek assistance in effecting our purpose. I agreed, and later that day the Cabinet of Barbados decided to support a multi-national intervention in Grenada after Caribbean Leaders had had an opportunity of discussing the situation and of jointly initiating action.

The OECS countries and Jamaica, however, all came to Barbados on the Friday October 21. During that day I saw the diplomatic representatives of four countries. I first saw the High Commissioner for Trinidad and Tobago and explained to him, in confidence for transmission to his Prime Minister, that I would be unable to attend the Caribbean heads of government the next day in Trinidad since a military intervention in Grenada was being contemplated by the OECS with Barbados and other countries, in which the participation of all CARICOM countries would be invited. I told him that my presence would be absolutely necessary in Barbados to conduct negotiations with countries taking part, and also to take such decisions on the military details as fell to the Chairman of the Defence Board.

At 12.30 p.m. I saw the British High Commissioner and told him also what was contemplated and that Britain would be invited to participate. I next saw the United States Ambassador and told him the same thing and that an invitation was likely to be extended to Britain. He undertook to convey the facts to President Reagan while awaiting a formal request should one be issued.

At 5 p.m. I saw the High Commissioner for Canada at his request, and discussed the situation in Grenada generally. He gave me the views of his Prime Minister and I responded. Although it had not been contemplated by those of us who had discussed the matter that Canada would have been invited, in deference to the outstandingly close relations of Canada and Barbados and the very high regard I have for Prime Minister Trudeau, I did tell the High Commissioner that my view of the Grenada situation was that the only solution was a military intervention.

That evening the OECS, Antigua and Barbuda, Dominica, St. Kitts-Nevis, St. Lucia, St. Vincent and the Grenadines, with Montserrat held a meeting — first a formal meeting of their Ministers of Defence and then a meeting of their governing Authority, and unanimously agreed to invoke Article 8 of their Treaty of Association and to seek the assistance of friendly countries to stabilise the situation and to establish a peacekeeping force. It is important to note that neither Grenada nor any Eastern Caribbean country, including Barbados, although members of the Organisation of American States, are signatories of the 1947 Rio Treaty and that the OAS is therefore ruled out as a peacekeeping body in our immediate area.

I was requested to attend the OECS meeting and issued with an invitation for Barbados to participate. I agreed within the terms of our Cabinet's decision. Troop numbers were settled and the staff of the Regional Security Organisation of which Barbados and most of the Eastern Caribbean States are members were deputed to do the necessary military planning.

I was then deputed by the OECS, formally to notify Britain and the United States, through their local diplomatic representatives of the decision and to make known our wish for their participation in the multi-national force.

Later that evening, Prime Minister Eugenia Charles and I met Prime Minister Seaga of Jamaica, who on behalf of Jamaica accepted the invitation to participate, and jointly we formally invited the participation of the US through its Ambassador whom I saw for a second time.

Next day, Saturday, October 22, I saw Prime Minister Price of Belize, who indicated that he did not wish to participate and could not in any event without the consent of the British Government, make any military commitment for Belize. I again saw the British High Commissioner and made a fully formal verbal request, indicating that a document of invitation would follow. This document was eventually delivered on Monday morning.

Meanwhile, in Port-of-Spain, the remaining Heads of Government were informed and a long and inconclusive debate ensued on the night of Saturday, October 22, until after 2 a.m. I made contact between 2 a.m. and 4 a.m. in the morning with a number of the Heads and when the meeting resumed on Sunday morning the subject was not discussed further. Instead, by a majority of 11 to 1, the Heads agreed on sanctions against Grenada and to refer an agreed proposal for restructuring CARICOM to include human rights and democracy qualifications and to remove the strict unanimity rule in some areas, to the Regions Attorneys-General for advice on how to effectuate it. The sole dissenter, Guyana, indicated that it would not wish to participate in CARICOM II.

To the foregoing narrative should be added one major theme which ran through all the planning. At all points it was agreed that the Governor-General of Grenada was the only constitutional authority remaining in the country and the only one who, in addition to any treaty rights which might and did exist, could issue a formal invitation to foreign countries to enter Grenada to restore order.

Accordingly, the participating countries have had no difficulty in deciding that he should be invested with formal authority as soon as his person should be secured — and this was made a number one priority at operation level.

Now that Sir Paul Scoon is safe, I can reveal that by the kind offices of a friendly government, albeit non-participating government, his views were sought well before the military operations commenced on the issuing of an invitation of friendly countries to enter Grenada and restore order. According to my information Sir Paul agreed to do so as soon as possible. He has now given his sanction and Brigadier Lewis is in possession of his signed letter of invitation to the OECS and other participating governments.

On Monday night at 8.10 the American Ambassador attended my residence and read out to me a formal note from President Reagan indicating that the United States would accept the invitation of the Organisation of Eastern Caribbean States and participate in the intervention in Grenada. The intervention proceeded and has been successful.

The pros and cons of the actions of the Caribbean Governments will long be debated. So will those of President Reagan in coming to our aid. But I think that history will agree with the verdict of public opinion in the Eastern Caribbean. There has seldom in these islands been such virtually unanimous support in the media and at political and popular level for an action so potentially divisive. West Indians have shown that we have a view of our future that is democratic, peace-loving, devoted to constitutional and not arbitrary government. We have shown that we can cut through the sometimes artificial controversies generated by today's media and go right to the heart of things — what is best for our people. The United States and President Reagan have to their eternal credit come to the same conclusion as we have.

ORGANISATION OF EASTERN CARIBBEAN STATES:
PRESS RELEASE
of 31 October, 1983

Source: Secretariat of the Organisation of Eastern Caribbean States,
Castries, St. Lucia

The Authority of the Organisation of Eastern Caribbean States met in Special Session on Saturday, October 29, 1983 in Barbados, to review the situation in Grenada subsequent to the entry of the multinational military force into that country. The Heads of Government of Barbados and Jamaica, also participated in this meeting on the invitation of the Authority.

The Heads of Government discussed the military situation in Grenada up to that time, and subsequent arrangements which would have to be made to consolidate the successes of the multinational force and to maintain law and order and public security in Grenada in the future. Consideration was given to the necessity for arranging for adequate peacekeeping and police forces in Grenada.

The Heads of Government expressed strong concern at the extensive quantity of military equipment discovered in Grenada by the multinational force, and saw this as further evidence in support of their earlier claims of the serious threat posed to the peace and security of the sub-region involving foreign elements.

The Heads of Government noted that the Director-General had, at the invitation of the Governor-General of Grenada visited Grenada on Friday 28th October for discussions; and that the Prime Minister of Barbados had also had discussions with the Governor-General on Saturday 29th October. The Heads of Government discussed the question of appropriate constitutional arrangements for Grenada, noting with satisfaction that the Governor-General of Grenada had now assumed executive authority for the management of the affairs of the country, and had announced his intention to establish an interim administration pending the holding of general elections towards the re-establishment of constitutional rule in Grenada.

Heads of Government agreed, in the light of the present situation, to remove the sanctions which had been imposed on Grenada on Friday 21st October 1983. In this context, it was agreed that LIAT could resume its normal operations into Pearl's airport, Grenada, on Monday 31st October, subject to the lifting of the 60 mile zone military prohibition.

They took note of the announcement by the Governor-General of Grenada that he had informed the Secretary-General of the United Nations that no one had the right at present to represent Grenada in international institutions and agreed that, subject to the advice of the Governor-General, there would be no cooperation in such institutions by the member-states of the Organisation with persons claiming to represent Grenada.

Heads of Government received reports on the state of the public utilities and the food supply situation in Grenada. They agreed to help the authorities in Grenada in seeking assistance for restoring the utilities and arranging for emergency food supplies to that country.

Heads of Government agreed that it was desirable for representatives of the International Red Cross to enter Grenada to provide appropriate assistance.

Heads of Government further agreed to express their deep appreciation to the Government of the United States of America for the services being rendered by the United States Armed Forces, and expressed sympathy to the families of those who had been killed, wounded or are missing in action.

APPENDIX NO. 13

GENERAL ASSEMBLY RESOLUTION 38/7
RELATING TO THE SITUATION IN GRENADA
of 2 November, 1983

Source: United Nations Information Centre, London, U.K.

The General Assembly,

Considering the statements made before the Security Council in connection with the situation in Grenada,

Recalling the Declaration on Principles of International Law concerning Friendly Relations and Co-operation among States in accordance with the Charter of the United Nations, 1/

Recalling also the Declaration on the Inadmissibility of Intervention and Interference in the Internal Affairs of States, 2/

Reaffirming the sovereign and inalienable right of Grenada freely to determine its own political, economic and social system, and to develop its international relations without outside intervention, interference, subversion, coercion or threat in any form whatsoever,

1/ Resolution 2625 (XXV), annex.
2/ Resolution 36/103, annex.

Deeply deploring the events in Grenada which led to the killing of the Prime Minister, Mr. Maurice Bishop, and other prominent Grenadians,

Bearing in mind that, in accordance with Article 2, paragraph 4, of the Charter of the United Nations, all Member States are obliged to refrain in their international relations from the threat or use of force against the territorial integrity or political independence of any State or in any other manner inconsistent with the principles of the Charter,

Gravely concerned at the military intervention taking place and determined to ensure a speedy return to normalcy in Grenada,

Conscious of the need for States to show consistent respect for the principles of the Charter,

1. *Deeply deplores* the armed intervention in Grenada, which constitutes a flagrant violation of international law and of the independence, sovereignty and territorial integrity of that State;

2. *Deplores* the death of innocent civilians resulting from the armed intervention;

3. *Calls upon* all States to show the strictest respect for the sovereignty, independence and territorial integrity of Grenada;

4. *Calls for* an immediate cessation of the armed intervention and the immediate withdrawal of the foreign troops from Grenada;

5. *Requests* that free elections be organized as rapidly as possible to enable the people of Grenada to choose its government democratically;

6. *Requests* the Secretary-General as a matter of urgency to assess the situation and to report back to the General Assembly within seventy-two hours.

43rd plenary meeting
2 November 1983

SPEECH BY PRIME MINISTER ADAMS OF BARBADOS
TO THE ROYAL COMMONWEALTH SOCIETY, LONDON (EXTRACTS)
of 9 December, 1983

Source: High Commission for Barbados, London, U.K.

Those of us in the Caribbean who had been very concerned over the March 1979 revolution had begun learning to live with the *de facto* situation in Grenada. Many people had begun to discern what the New York Times called "a drift towards moderation", and I might mention that I never saw any hint in the New Jewel Movement of the ideological divisions at work which finally consumed Maurice Bishop and Party alike. The shock of the house arrests and the eventual murder of the moderate leadership came like a series of bolts from the blue.

Against this background the Prime Minister of St. Lucia contacted me and pointed out that the situation in Grenada could not remain as it was. He argued powerfully that in the interest of the Eastern Caribbean on the whole it was necessary for Caribbean countries to intervene to restore law and order and return the country to democracy. He sought Barbados' assistance and on that same day our Cabinet agreed to support a multinational intervention in Grenada after Caribbean Leaders had had an opportunity of discussing the situation and jointly initiating action.

The countries of the Eastern Caribbean including Grenada are all members of the Organisation of Eastern Caribbean States, Article 8 of whose embodying treaty authorises certain actions to preserve security. On this basis the OECS Heads of Government held a formal meeting at which they unanimously agreed to invoke Article 8. The Heads were obviously aware that, since Grenada under the New Jewel Movement had been turned into an armed camp, the rest of the OECS even with the resources of the Regional Security Organisation to which most of them belonged would not be able to subdue the Revolutionary Military Council and restore order in the island. They accordingly invited Jamaica, Barbados and other countries, including the United States and Britain, to participate in an intervention in Grenada for this purpose. Further, Government having been destroyed in Grenada itself the Governor-General became the Constitutional Authority in the island who could formally invite foreign countries to enter and restore order. His opinion and approval were obtained, and arrangements made for him to issue a formal invitation as soon as it was physically safe for him to do so. In advance of a formal reply to the OECS invitation, officers from the United States of America joined with officers from Jamaica and from the Regional Security Organisation

109

which consisted of Antigua and Barbuda, Barbados, Dominica, St. Lucia and St. Vincent in planning an operation. St. Kitts-Nevis, which is in the process of joining the Regional Security Grouping, made arrangements to contribute a contingent, but Montserrat, which is still an Associated State, was prevented by the U.K. Government from participating on an officially organised basis. Caribbean forces were assembled in Barbados, and a United States task force on its way to the Mediterranean was diverted to the Caribbean. No reply on participation was ever received by the OECS from Britain itself, but the USA responded on October 24th and on the morning of October 25th a landing was effected in Grenada.

Post facto justifications for an action as fraught with implications as the Grenada intervention are of course dangerous. But given what is, as I have said, the virtually unique character of the operation, it should surely be repeated in its favour that it was viewed by the population as a liberation, an "invasion" only in the sense that the invasion of Normandy in 1944 was an invasion. The discovery of a sufficient store of ammunition to kill everyone in the Caribbean and of weapons and equipment not only of defensive but with an offensive capacity will surely raise the question of the past Government's intentions. Why did Grenada need motorised rubber landing craft? What would it have done with the fifty Armoured Personnel Carriers it had agreed to obtain from the Soviet Union, a number probably greater than that possessed by all CARICOM Armies combined? I have recently looked at a just published World Human Rights Guide which among other things analyses the extent of militarisation in countries. Grenada, already under Bishop one of the perhaps dozen most militarised states in the world in terms of population under arms, would have become the most militarised if plans to expand the People's Revolutionary Army had gone through in terms of Agreements already signed. Can all these factors be ignored in assessing the threat posed to Eastern Caribbean Countries against which their Treaty entitles them to defend themselves?

Publications of the author

"Newfoundland Offshore Minerals", 7 Marine Policy (1983)

"The Acquisition of Dominion Statehood Reconsidered", 22 Virginia Journal of International Law (1982)

"Requiem for Associated Statehood?", 8 Review of International Studies (1982)

"The Anguilla Act, 1980: A Question of Constitutional Propriety", (1981) West Indian Law Journal

"Newfoundland and the League of Nations", XVIII Canadian Yearbook of International Law (1980)

"Legal Perspectives on Associated Statehood in the Eastern Caribbean", 19 Virginia Journal of International Law (1979)

"The Associated States of the Commonwealth Caribbean: The Constitution and the Individual", 11 Lawyer of the Americas (1979)

"Perspectives on Abortion Law Reform in Barbados", 8 Anglo-American Law Review (1979)

"Belligerent Occupation, Public Property and War Crimes in Namibia: A New Role for International Law", 11 Current Comment (1976)

"The Suppression of Crime (Special Provisions) Act 1974: A Suitable Case for Treatment", (1975) Jamaica Law Journal

Short notes and comments in (1975) and (1983) Juridical Review; 4 International Trade Law Journal (1978); House of Commons Paper 47 (1981-82), Appendix 26.

"The Grenada Intervention: Analysis and Documentation", published as a monograph by Berlin Verlag Arno Spitz, Berlin 33, and Mansell Publishing Ltd., London

Forthcoming Publications

"The Search for Constitutional Change in the U.S. Virgin Islands" — forthcoming in Social and Economic Studies

The External Affairs Competence and International Law Status of Newfoundland, 1855-1934; "Legal Aspects of Sub-Regional Integration in the Eastern Caribbean" (for the 1985 volume of Review of International Studies)

Unpublished Works

A Summary of Significant Events in the Evolution of Newfoundland's Separate International Personality (A 186 page work submitted under the name of the Attorney General of Newfoundland as Part II of his Factum, in a Reference by the Lieutenant-Governor in Council, to the Supreme Court of Newfoundland, Court of Appeal Division, in September 1982. Resubmitted under the same title and in substantially similar form as Appendix A of the Factum of the Attorney General of Newfoundland, in a Reference by the Governor in Council, to the Supreme Court of Canada in November 1982)

"Legal Problems in the Arctic with Special Reference to Canada: A paper presented to the Royal Institute of International Affairs, 6 November, 1982

"The Role of the U.K. Parliament and the Patriation of the Canadian Constitution": Paper presented to a seminar at the Centre for Canadian Studies, University of Edinburgh, 14 March, 1981

"Sugar and Agricultural Diversification in the Barbadian Economy", M.A. Thesis, Carleton University, Ottawa, March, 1977 (pass with distinction)

Educational Data

1983 - present:	PhD/MPhil, external candidate, University of London, England
1980:	M.A. (International Affairs/Development Studies), Carleton University, Ottawa, Canada
1972:	LL.M (Public International Law), University College of the University of London, London, England
1971:	LL.B (Law), University of Edinburgh, Edinburgh, Scotland

ABBREVIATIONS

CARICOM	Caribbean Community and Common Market
CEPAL	Economic Commission for Latin America
ECCA	East Caribbean Currency Authority
ECCB	East Caribbean Central Bank
ECCM	East Caribbean Common Market
GDP	Gross Domestic Product
ILC	International Law Commission
LDC	Less Developed Countries
MAP	Master Assembly for the People
OAS	Organization of American States
OECS	Organization of Eastern Caribbean States
PRG	People's Revolutionary Government
RMC	Revolutionary Military Council
WISA	West Indies (Associated States) Council of Ministers